Lu

and the

Holy Spirit

Maria Isabel Pita

Copyright © 2015 by Maria Isabel Pita
All rights reserved.

ISBN: 978-150892-605-4

Printed in the U.S.A. by Create Space

Contents

Introduction - Cathedral in the Mist.................................1
Chapter One - A Great Wind..7
   Shadow People..10
   A Conversation...14
   Cared For..16
   Weighing of the Heart 20
Chapter Two - Struggles..29
   Indoctrination...29
   Deception..32
   The Man Upstairs...35
   Vanity...36
Chapter Three - Dreams of Christmas................................41
   A Sign...41
   Teacher..44
      Healing My Tendinitis in Lucid Dreams...................48
   Glass Bus..54
   A Prayer...57
Chapter Four - The Lord is With Us.................................61
   Triptych...61
   Waiting and Wanting..66
   Rescued..70
   Purification 74
Chapter Five - Communicating.......................................77
   The Kiss...78
      Dream Sharing...80
   Divine Speech..85
      Telepathic and Precognitive Dreams......................89
   Following Him..93
Chapter Six - Engaged..99
   The Book of Life...99
   Re-Confirmation...107
   Heavenly Games..111
   An Invitation 114
Chapter Seven - The Holy Spirit...................................123

- Inspiration..125
- The Bread of Life..133
- The Holy Spirit...136

Chapter Eight - Buried Treasure.............................145
- Mary and Elizabeth..145
- The Battle..149
- Angels Sing..152
- Christmas Is Coming..154

Chapter Nine - The King's Chamber........................159
- Talking to my Lord About Lucid Dreaming...............159
- Breath of Life...162
- In His Company..167
- Faith...172

Chapter Ten - Upheld..177
- Martyrs 177
- Light and Shadow...179
- God's Protection...189
- Beloved...195

Chapter Eleven - Purification..................................203
- Maid of Honor..203
- Day by Day..208
- Taking Out the Trash...209
- Dancing With the Prince.....................................213

Chapter Twelve - Discernment................................219
- Appearances..219
- The Comforter..222
- Where Did Abuela Go?!......................................225
- Get Thee Behind Me Satan..................................230

Chapter Thirteen – Love in Action............................235
- The Forces of Light..235
- The Embracing Tree 240
- Christ's Hospital..246

Chapter Fourteen - Thresholds................................251
- Miriam..251
- Love and Courage...253
- Midnight Prayer and the Holy Spirit......................255

Afterword..257
- The Mystery of Norwich Street.............................257

Acknowledgments..263

About the Author..265
End Notes..266

Introduction – Cathedral in the Mist

The term "Lucid Dreaming" is relatively new, but there is evidence the phenomena is as old as humanity. A lucid dream occurs when you become aware of the fact that you are dreaming, and fully conscious of the experience even though your body is asleep.

The first lucid dream I remember having, two decades before I began intentionally incubating lucid dreams, was when I was twenty-two years old and living on the rebellious edge in Chicago. I dreamed I was walking through an empty parking lot, where I stopped to buy ice cream from a vendor. I handed him some money, and he returned my change. "This is too much," I protested, but he insisted I keep it. I knew then I was dreaming, because in real life no one gives you money. I shrugged, slipped the $5 bill into the right pocket of my black jacket, and woke up.

Less than twenty minutes later, just after sunrise, I was leaning against the wall of a fast food restaurant, waiting for a friend to pick me up as I stared despondently across a mostly empty parking lot. A slender black man with a kind face paused beside me, asked me if I was hungry, and offered to buy me breakfast. When he handed me his card, I realized he was a social worker. I smiled, and told him I was fine. He said, "Well, if you won't join me for breakfast, at least buy yourself something to eat" as he slipped a bill into the right pocket of my jacket, the same jacket I had been wearing in the dream. I waited until he had entered the restaurant before pulling out the money. It was a $5 bill.

I will never forget that morning. I felt I had been given a clear message – dreams can and do come true, *believe* it.

I have been lucid dreaming on a consistent basis, at least five times a month, for more than four years. I feel, I *know*, there is a spiritual dimension to lucid dreaming that transcends the mere sport of it.

I embrace both fully lucid dreams, and what I call semi-lucid dreams, in my practice. Semi-lucid dreams are often much more profoundly affecting to me than many of my lucid dreams. In semi-lucid dreams, I am in full possession of my faculties, I just don't have that "aha, I'm dreaming" moment, and I feel strongly that it's because I don't want, or need, to have it.

I was raised Catholic, but only went to Sunday School for one year when I was still too young to remember any of it. All my life I attended public schools, except for in seventh and eighth grade, when I went to St. Leo's in Fairfax, Virginia. I have always felt a deep love for Christ, and even though, as an adult, I became detached from my Christianity, I never stopped believing in the Divinity of Christ, who was always there in the back of my mind, secreted away in my heart.

It was not until *after* I dreamed the dreams in this book—in one of which I was gently but firmly told, "Don't be silly, read your leaders"—that I began avidly reading the works of certain Christian mystics. It had been decades since I even looked at a Bible, of which I had only ever read brief excerpts from the four Gospels, along with a handful of stories from the Old Testament, specifically the ones about interesting women such as Ruth and

Esther.

The lucid and semi-lucid dreams set down here cannot simply be dismissed as conscious or subconscious reflections of religious and mystical experiences I was already intimately familiar with. Not understanding the Holy Trinity, I did not know that it was possible to experience God personally.

The seed of my mysteriously seductive relationship with the Holy Spirit was planted five years ago. At the age of forty-nine, eight years into my first truly happy relationship, my husband and I moved to Virginia, where I had grown up and ached to return. We desired to live surrounded by nature, with just enough land for privacy and to grow vegetables.

We made an offer on a house in the Blue Ridge mountains, and the following afternoon, we drove eagerly back to see what would soon (we fervently hoped) be our home for the rest of our lives. It was mid-February, the weather was gray, drizzling rain, and the mountain top was shrouded in mist. We were hoping the ice-covered driveway winding up to the house would have thawed, but it hadn't, so I parked beside the mailbox, and sat in the car as my husband skated up the frozen path to inspect the property.

The mist obscured the trees in a haunting way I was thoroughly savoring. Then slowly, and yet somehow also suddenly, I perceived a slender structure rising between a group of trees just above me on an ascending slope... a Cathedral. I studied the tall, narrow front doors with pleasure, waiting for the illusion to vanish. But even after I looked away, and then back again, several times, the Cathedral remained distinctly there, so much so that I was able to study architectural features of the wooden door frame, which was sharply arched on top. I saw, and also felt, the intimate Cathedral's presence.

When our offer on the house was accepted, I found myself imagining that when I died, my spirit would rise out of my body and float through the woods to the Cathedral I had seen in the mist, the doors of which I would, at long last, have the power to open as I crossed the threshold into the next world...

Less than a year after we moved in, I discovered, and avidly began reading, Robert Waggoner's book *Lucid Dreaming: Gateway to the Inner Self.* Before I even finished it, I had the lucid dream which began my spiritual practice. I know now that I was blessed by my vision of a Cathedral in the mist, that it was a sign of what was to come.

Each of the chapters in this book features relevant dreams in the order I experienced them. The end of each dream is indicated by a black star ★ usually followed by what I wrote about my dream the next day preceded by the heading: *That morning I wrote.* A half moon ◐ indicates where I begin speaking about the dream in the present tense.

The verses at the beginning of each chapter are from an ever growing body of prayer-poems I began in May of 2014. The poems appear in the order they were written.

In both the Old and New Testaments, dreams are privileged ways in which God communicates with people.[1]

There are four distinct ways of looking at the process of spiritual formation... The third perspective, more feminine in its tone and experience, is the way of spiritual espousal and often employs bridal imagery. Here, spiritual formation is experienced as God the lover seducing, wooing and trying to win the heart of the beloved who is the believer."[2]

Chapter One – A Great Wind

Planting vegetables in our garden
the morning after a lucid dream
I felt how sunlight is God's power
and water His love for everything

I had the following dream early in 2009. I did not even bother to write it down because I knew I would never forget it:

I am sitting in a dark stone cellar or tomb. A darkly tanned man is lying beside me on a stone bed wrapped in a white sheet, oddly immobile even though his eyes are open, and I distinctly feel the power of his consciousness. On the black wall beside him hang three dark-gray masks with empty eye sockets that look ancient, and yet also somehow timeless. I am sitting right next to him, and I know he will soon rise again. In preparation for this, I ascend a narrow stairwell to the ground floor of a large white unfurnished house with glass walls.

I am followed by a procession of people, both men and women, all of us dressed in colorful flowing garments. Like the point of an arrowhead, I lead the way to the front of the house, two rows of kindred spirits fanning out behind me. We take positions in front of the glass walls, which may as well not be there—our hair and clothing stream behind us from the force of the wind blowing, from every direction, straight toward us across a hazy twilight landscape of green fields, forests and mountains. It is a dangerously powerful wind, but my soul exults in it.

I didn't realize it at the time, but this dream was when it all began for me, more than two years before I began lucid dreaming regularly, and intelligently. Before I read Robert Waggoner's book, the occasional times I "woke up" in a dream, I invariably began flying. I had never even heard the term "lucid dreaming" and I called them "flying dreams" because that was the first thing I did when I became lucid. During these early lucid dreams I barely scratched the surface of lucidity—I didn't realize I could do anything besides feel fantastic and invulnerable. These dreams were also akin to sightseeing tours, because I would fly over whole towns and cities and landscapes and see them in such vivid detail, it made me want to cry when I woke up that I couldn't remember everything more clearly.

This dream, brief but powerful, is an example of what I referred to in the Introduction as a semi-lucid dream. When I woke up, I felt exhilarated, but really didn't know what to make of it. The man, wrapped tightly up in a white shroud, I simply filed under one of my favorite headings, "ancient Egypt." I had, after all, just finished writing a massive fictional biography of the female pharaoh, Hatshepsut-Maatkare. I thought that perhaps the man in my dream represented one of the great kings of pre-dynastic Egypt.

In college, I minored in cultural Anthropology, while doing a double major in World History and English Literature, and from a very young age, I had spent hours devouring books about ancient civilizations. The three powerfully enigmatic masks, which I saw hanging above the man in my dream, had looked and felt almost impossibly old, but thinking about them when I woke up, I couldn't place them in any historical time period and culture I was familiar with. I certainly had no clue how the masks might relate to the wind in my dream, which had made me feel that something transcendent was heading my way.

I felt this wind was much more than just the proverbial wind of change blowing through my personal life—my husband and I were preparing to sell our house and move to another State—as well as through the political life of the country with a new president in office.

At the time, I could not connect the different pieces of the dream together in a way that completely worked, and truly satisfied me. Now I understand that the man wrapped in a white shroud and lying in a stone tomb, from which I knew he would soon rise again, represented Christ. The awesome, timeless mystery of the three masks was the Holy Trinity, and the wind that made me feel so intensely alive and hopeful, poised on the brink of a life-changing event, was the Holy Spirit, beginning to blow through my dreams into my soul.

Shadow People

Dream of February 5, 2011

At around 5:30 a.m., I'm lying in bed, in a state somewhere on the cusp of waking and sleeping consciousness, observing vividly detailed scenes—which are not of my own imagining—appearing before my closed eyelids. (*At the time I did not know the term for this phenomena: Hypnagogic[3] Imagery*). With an effort of will, I hold onto one of these scenes, and prevent it from fading by becoming part of it. I am in what feels, and appears to be, a subterranean train station. I get the sense that where I am, not conscious of a body, only of my awareness of being in a dream, there is a train track. For a few moments, I focus on the back concrete wall, discerning metal fixtures of some kind. In the foreground, there is a row of people whose faces I see clearly... until I become aware of shadowy figures to their left.

I'm not sure if I actually speak out loud when I ask, "Are you afraid of the spirits of the dead?" as my awareness shifts further left to the people standing in shadow. I get a strong, creepy feeling observing the way absolute darkness covers their upper bodies, exposing only the bottom halves of heavy dark winter clothing. My first reaction is to turn away from them toward the "living" people, but I remember that in a lucid dream I should face what frightens me.

I can faintly but distinctly sense my physical body lying in bed, and how tenuous my presence in this lucid dream is, but I am determined to hold onto it. I begin "floating" along the row of shadowy presences. As I do so, their entire bodies are revealed to me, but their faces are wrapped in dark, grayish cloths that mask their features and expose only their eyes. One woman I focus on —sending reassuring thought-feelings her way—stares avidly back at me as I silently communicate to her that I'm not afraid of them; that I don't think they are all inherently evil. Her eyes seem to smile gratefully in response, but then she begins to blur.

Remembering a technique commonly used to hold on to a lucid dream when it begins dissolving, I make a concerted effort to lift my hands in front of my face, and as I do so, I feel my physical hands on the bed trying to rise. With an effort of will, I succeed in perceiving an out of focus version of what I know must be my hands.

As my awareness continues "floating" to the left in front of the platform, I look back up at the row of people. When I reach the end of the line, I drift closer to a female figure whose wintery layers of clothing look especially sad and wretched. I say out loud, speaking in Spanish with quiet urgency, "¿Quién eres? ¿Quién eres?" ("Who are you? Who are you?")

Moving back and beginning to fade into the darkness behind her, she replies, "Soy de tu niñez." ("I am from your childhood.")

Surprised, and yet not surprised by her response, I wish I could have gotten more from her as I begin floating to the right. Quickly passing another figure, I demand, "Who are you!?" but then murmur an apology, realizing that my authoritative tone is not the way to approach them.

Suddenly, a tall man—who was not part of the line-up of

people, moves toward me—His body is concealed by a long black coat that looks much more affluent than what the others are wearing, and even though I can't see his face, I get the feeling he is fair-skinned and has reddish hair.

Firmly but not unkindly, he commands, "Keep moving forward."

I obey him simply by not backing away as he walks straight into me, and as my face merges with his chest, I experience what I can only describe as a surge of energy flowing up my spine.

The dream begins to fade as I drift further to the right, still facing the platform lined with people. The fade-to-gray happens gradually before I "land" back in my body on the bed.

I thought about this dream a lot, and about the woman who told me, "I am from your childhood." I was born in Havana, Cuba on February 9, 1961, during a period of violent turmoil. My father was involved in the resistance against the totalitarian regime being imposed on Cubans, and was forced to take refuge in the Brazilian Embassy. He would stand at the wrought iron fence while my mother, holding me in her arms, walked back and forth along the sidewalk so he could at least *see* his baby.

When I was four months old, Mami and I flew to Madrid, and for approximately four months we lived in the convent school *Our Lady of Victories*, run by Sisters who belonged to the same denomination as the school my mother attended most of her life, *Our Lady of Lourdes*. While we were in residence there, the two young nuns who helped care for me—one of whom rocked me to sleep every night—drowned in a boating accident. The story haunted me as a child; I felt bound to these young Sisters in some mysterious way. My family reunited in Miami, where my sister and brother were born, but when my father was offered a job with U.S.A.I.D., we moved to Fairfax, Virginia, where I lived until I was seventeen. My maternal grandparents lived with us, and my grandmother was essentially our nanny. At first we were brutally poor, but I was too young to notice, being rich in love.

After this, my first truly lucid dream, I wondered if, while listening as a child to stories about Cuba and relatives still imprisoned there, I might have absorbed more painful emotions than I realized and consciously dealt with. That was the psychological perspective on my dream, but it didn't feel right. The poverty I perceived in the row of shadow people was, I distinctly felt, a spiritual poverty.

It seems to me that those figures on the platform—wrapped in the darkness of moral evil—embodied aspects of my personality I am still less than proud of, bad habits, tendencies, prejudices and fears I am consciously striving to leave behind, while at the same time not judging myself too harshly; trying not to feel too guilty about how long it has taken me to face them.

In hindsight, I can see how the people standing in the light, on the right side of the platform, represented souls who have heard God's Word and embraced Christ.

When the man who was obviously in command of the scene walked into me, I experienced a surge of energy I now feel transformed me in some mysteriously positive way, quite literally overnight, making it possible for me to "keep moving forward" in a new direction, away from the worldly track I had, in too many respects, been blindly following.

I feel as though I received something; as though something entered into me. This dream initiated my lucid dreaming practice; after that night, I began lucid dreaming regularly. I feel this dream was a blessing, and certainly my life has not been the same since.

A Conversation

Dream of February 14, 2011

I'm standing beside a small run down and sparsely furnished house which I also sense doubles as a business. There are two rooms, in one of which a man is telling me that I'm welcome to stay for the season because the owner doesn't occupy it. I find the prospect rather bleak as I regard the room from outside it, standing in some larger space that seems to be half outdoors and half indoors. I really don't know why he thinks I would want to rent such a cramped and cheerless space.

Then another older man, who is standing slightly to my right, asks me, "How did you get here?" He sounds surprised, and maybe a little suspicious.

Abruptly, I realize I'm dreaming. I've made it into a lucid dream! "I came here on my own," I tell him proudly, but then add a little more humbly, "I've been reading some books about it and following some of the suggestions" so he won't think I'm an irresponsible fly-by-night lucid dreamer; I want him to know I'm a serious beginner.

Blended now with my determination to hold onto the dream is the knowledge that trying too hard will make it slip away, and that I should address the dream directly instead of a dream character. I really don't have a specific question to ask, so I simply look up and say, "If you show me something I need to see or hear, I will strive to use it to become a better, wiser person." I think I sound a little too much like a timid Catholic school girl, but that's how it came out.

I'm surprised when it's the dream character who responds, and he is no longer old; he is now a very handsome man with dark hair. Sitting on the bottom edge of what looks like a giant picture frame, he says, "I don't care too much for definitions. It's the personal experience that matters."

This makes perfect sense to me, and I ask him eagerly, "Love?"

"Love," he confirms, grinning at me.

I ask hopefully, "Merlin?" (*my recently deceased dog.*)

He echoes, "Merlin."

I add, "Even though he's just a dog?"

"Even though he's just a dog."

I realize then that I'm being silly; I'm not getting anymore from him because I shouldn't be asking the obvious. Of course it's all about love.

He stands up, and as he begins walking away, I follow him. I don't want to leave the dream so soon and so I ask him, "Can I stay for a while and just play?"

Still smiling, he makes a gesture with his right arm that translates into, "Knock yourself out."

The scene has expanded to a city block of sorts, but the architecture is such that the blue sky is visible and accessible through all the buildings. I immediately raise my arms and take off, flying fast, for even if I hit a wall, I'm confident I'll go safely through it. I'm exultant, because I haven't had a fun flying lucid dream in a long time. I soon wake.

That morning I wrote: I've read that some dream characters seem to act as what might be called Lucid Guardians, appearing to people who have recently embarked on the quest of becoming lucid in their dreams. Like last night, when the man asked me, "How did you get here?" which forced me to think about it, which made me lucid. And then he transformed into someone else entirely, a Person I felt could answer all my questions about everything. This young man had such a sweet, knowing smile, and I was perfectly comfortable in his presence.

Cared For

Dream of February 18, 2011

I both feel myself, and look down at my body, lying on a bed in a small room located on the upper floor of a house. My blankets are thrown off, and my eyes are closed, but I'm not asleep. The man I first saw wrapped in a white shroud—tall, handsome and very much alive now in an elegant black suit—walks into the room.

Losing the bird's eye view of the dream, I fully enter my body lying on the bed, and distinctly feel it when He gently pulls the blanket back over me, and then gently caresses my forehead. I sense how special I am to Him, how drawn He is to me, just as I am irresistibly drawn to Him.

Overwhelmed by how intensely we love each other, I am unable to move, feeling that, for some reason, our relationship has to remain a secret. And yet His appearance in my bedroom seems to prove there really *is* a connection between us, which makes me incredibly happy.

I wake up feeling just as I did in the dream, watched over, mysteriously cared for, but now also suddenly bereft. I don't know where that room or that house are, so how can I ever find Him?!

I treasured this special little dream, even as it deeply saddened me to think that I would never in waking reality feel as I had when this man—who I had distinctly felt was no ordinary dream character—entered the bedroom of my dream, and covered me up against the cold like a father does his child. There was so much promise in the way he caressed my forehead, so much gentle longing... my emotions got tangled around my thoughts every time I remembered His touch.

How could I love a complete stranger so much? Who was he?

How could I live without him? Was he a real man I was destined to meet? That seemed impossible, and not at all desirable, because I was very much in love with my husband. Besides, the all-consuming, timeless intensity of the love I had felt between this Person and my dreaming soul was light years beyond romantic—it was *everything*.

I couldn't wrap my brain around this dream, so I was obliged to simply file it away in the back of my mind, scarcely daring to hope this man would enter my dreams again.

I have known, ever since I was a little girl, that dreams do not happen merely in my own isolated brain. When I was eleven years old, my mother had a dream in which she saw a beloved friend of hers, a brilliant male surgeon, lying in a pool of blood. In her dream, a bicycle had fallen from the sky and crushed his skull. Then, on a large luminous white page, she saw a long poem written in English. It appeared before her so clearly, she was able to write it down when she woke up. The poem made reference to a tragic event which knowledge, time and love would transform into something beautiful. Less than two years later—even though she had never shown the slightest inclination toward becoming a writer—she published her first book of poems in Spanish. My mother, Juana Rosa Pita, is now considered one of Cuba's most important poets in exile, and has been translated into English and Italian.

Fifteen years after this dream, my mother was going through a pile of boxes and came across the dream poem which had transformed her life. That night, she dreamed with her surgeon friend again. She was standing at the railing of a ship, and he was leaning on the same railing facing her, suspended above the ocean. Smiling ruefully, he told her he would no longer be able to be her friend, that she would have to be *his* friend now. With that said, he plunged into the water and was lost.

The following morning, my mother received a phone call informing her that while her surgeon friend was leaving work the previous night, he was attacked by two assailants who hit him on the head thirteen times with metal bars. Miraculously, he survived. He was a very wealthy man, and he had been about to initiate a dream project of his—a large hospital ship that would cruise up and down the Nile river in his home country of Egypt, providing free medical care to the poor.

Suspecting someone had tried to have him killed, the police brought in a psychic to sit by his unconscious body in the hospital, where he was in a coma for twenty days. The only piece of information the psychic picked up from him was my mother's name, Juana Rosa. As it happens, my mother was the only one in the room with him when he finally opened his eyes. Seeing her, he grasped her hand, kissed it, and said, "Thank you" almost as if he knew that the first thing she had done upon arriving at the hospital was pour water from the holy shrine of Lourdes (brought to her from France by an acquaintance) over his forehead.

The case was never solved, but I had learned that dreams can transform you in dramatic, and seemingly magical, ways. I learned that in dreams time and space are somehow transcended, and that it's possible to communicate "telepathically" with other people. I learned that it's not a waste of time, that it's actually very important, to pay attention to our dreams and believe in them.

Weighing of the Heart

Dream of April 29, 2011

A lucid flash of an email from Sara (*a life-long friend who had passed away the previous month.*) I saw her message on my computer screen, and stared at it long and hard to confirm it was really there. Three previous emails were from my brother, but this new message was definitely from Sara...

My husband, Stinger, and I are sitting on the couch in the Den watching television. On the screen is a sexy film in which handsome men, wearing skimpy black leather outfits, smile and dance suggestively against the backdrop of a bar. I can't understand why we're watching something that doesn't appeal to either one of us.

I stand up, and between a gap in the green curtains hanging in front of the sliding glass doors, I glimpse a giant man striding across our property. He is wearing black leather, like the dancers in the film. I can scarcely believe my eyes when he abruptly strides in my direction, and slaps a piece of paper against the glass with the illustration facing me. I immediately recognize an ancient Egyptian scene as I make out two goddesses, and a third figure standing on the other side of the central object—the Scales of Maat, on which the heart of every human being was weighed after death against the feather that represented Truth. If the heart weighed more than the feather, it was thrown to the Devourer.

I glance over at Stinger and ask him, "Do you see it?!" and am amazed when he replies that he does. Suddenly, the curtains over the glass doors are open, and I realize with a shock that a crowd of people has gathered outside. Some are sitting right next to the doors, while dozens more nearly fill the brick courtyard. The scene has the feel of an impromptu outdoor event, and makes me very nervous. Where did all these people come from? And what are they doing here? The only thing I'm sure of is that I do *not* want Stinger to go outside and confront the trespassers, but he is determined to do so.

Reluctantly, I follow him out through the Sun Room. I remain in front of the open door while my husband, intent on protecting me, runs over to confront the giant man. Raising my right arm before me, my index finger pointing here and there, I begin reciting *The Charm of Making*, from the film *Excalibur*: "Breath of the Serpent, Spell of Death and Life, the Song of the Maker." I feel the need for magical protection in this otherworldly crowd, but the make-believe charm has no effect whatsoever. Catching sight of a hostile looking man holding a knife and swiftly approaching Stinger from behind, I cry out a warning to my husband, and point at his would be assailant, determined to zap him or maybe set him on fire, the way I did my purse recently in a lucid dream. Nothing happens and, losing sight of Stinger, I hastily retreat back inside.

Closing every door behind me, I hurry back into the Den. This must be a dream, a nightmare! I command myself to wake up, "Wake up! Wake up!" but I'm in deep, so deep it all feels unnervingly real. Well, if I'm dreaming, that means I'm not trapped; I can simply fly away. First, however, I need to prepare myself to fly through the walls, and away from this dangerous crowd. To this end, I go stand before a mirror, which is not there in waking reality. I let my hair down, and regard my reflection, meeting my own eyes, getting ready...

Abruptly, I hear someone enter the house through the Sun Room door. Hoping it's my husband, I run anxiously out into the living room. Wearing a bright white dress shirt over black slacks, a strikingly handsome blonde man steps out of the kitchen, and takes hold of me, firmly gripping my upper arms as he looks directly down into my eyes. His unusually luminous blue-green irises filling my vision, I have no desire to look away.

I ask him, "Is this a lucid dream? Am I lucid dreaming?" to which he replies, "You're very bright" as he sits me down in the closest leather armchair. He radiates authority, but I don't feel threatened by him, on the contrary. What I can only describe as a telepathic download of information then takes place as I "hear" him tell me that I behave much too passively toward my brother (his mental and emotional well-being) and that where my friend Sara is right now she is temporarily cut off from her memories of certain people, and I get the feeling they are good memories I am part of...

No longer in my living room, I am now sitting beside the blonde man in the front row of a small gathering. We are facing an open area that is quickly filling up with people. Their numbers are daunting, and I find myself disturbed by the aimless way they mill around. I have no idea what's going on. The only thing I'm absolutely sure of is that my companion is protecting me. His left arm is draped over my shoulders, and I am resting peacefully, safely against his chest. We are separated from the people by a low fence, behind which they are all being mysteriously corralled. Somehow, I begin to understand they are here for the "questioning," the first stage in a judgment of some kind.

A female "newscaster" sitting in a dark "press box" to my left—which is cut into an impenetrably black wall—is translating the proceedings, her outfit a dramatic geometric blend of red, black and white. Sitting up, I ask my Protector, "Why do you need a translator if this is the spirit world?" In response, he walks over to the press box, which vanishes. I say, "Did you do it for my benefit?" and he replies, "Yes" as I phase out of the dream into waking consciousness.

Walking through the living room the next day, I paused in the place where the blonde man with the luminous eyes took hold of me, and distinctly felt there really *had* been someone here with me last night. Then I noticed a shining gilded illustration of a golden-haired archangel I had found at a thrift store and which, even though it made my New Age brain feel self-conscious, I simply could not resist buying. I hung it on the inside of the front door when we moved in, and now I realized it would have been directly behind my protector's head as I stood facing him in the dream.

It also felt significant to me that, the day of the night I dreamed this, countless people had died suddenly in Alabama when killer tornadoes hit both major cities. Did this have anything to do with the crowds in my dream? It did not seem a coincidence that the frightening giant out in the courtyard had shown me an image of the ancient Egyptian weighing of the heart, which every deceased soul had to go through after death.

I thought about what my Protector had said to me, "You're very bright." My best friend, Sara, had just passed away, and I was constantly, with every other thought, broadcasting my love for her, telling her how much I loved her, and missed her; my emotions shouting out to her in the hope that her soul would hear me and feel my love wherever she was. My mind and heart were on fire with hope and fear, faith and despair, a spiritual conflict always simmering inside me stoked into a bonfire by my beloved friend's passing. Perhaps, I thought, this spiritual conflagration—burning the divine elements of love, hope and faith—was visible to some other souls who had just suddenly and unexpectedly passed away and who, like moths, were irresistibly drawn to it. So I reasoned, for the compliment "You're very bright" had also felt like a gentle warning.

Commonly reported in documented Near Death Experiences[4] are intense, powerful emotions which might include ecstasy and peace but also fear. A sudden, violent death experienced by someone with no faith in God, someone who believes that life and consciousness do not survive the physical body, may, at least initially, be a dark, frightening experience in which the love and faith I was beaming out to my late friend shone like the welcoming beam of a lighthouse.

I still think the people in my dream may have been some of the souls abruptly separated from their physical bodies by two deadly tornadoes. My dream began with the ancient Egyptian judgment of the dead, a clear indication of the theme of my dream, but with a vital difference—the difference made by Jesus. Forgiveness is possible if we truly repent in our heart and open it to faith in God, for love and compassion are the Law in a redeemed world of which Christ is Lord.

But how many of these storm victims didn't believe in God or in life after death? How many felt hopelessly disoriented, or perhaps even imagined they were only dreaming? How many realized they must be out of their physical body, but feared that once their brain fired its last electrical synapses their awareness would blink out?

In this dream, I appear to have been surrounded by souls lovingly herded together and cared for by the Presence who, it seems, deliberately placed himself in front of my illustration of an Archangel. He appeared to me in a brilliant white shirt, and beneath his golden hair, his eyes were more luminous than any I have ever seen, awake or asleep. This dream made me feel how close heaven and earth truly are.

What I did not know at the time, and which I only just discovered, is that the Archangel Michael assists souls at the hour of death. I had heard of the Archangel Michael, but knew next to nothing about him. At the time I had this dream, I reasoned that my Protector was telling me he was a Guide by placing himself in front of the illustration of an angel, knowing that, in the morning, I would put two and two together. It did not even remotely cross my mind that he could in fact be the Archangel Michael. It wasn't until recently, when I was browsing online for books about the lives of saints, that I came upon a book about the Archangel Michael. The description made me realize how ignorant I was about this Angel, and I was inspired to find out more about him. It may sound trite, but my heart skipped a beat when I read the following paragraph:

> In Roman Catholicism Saint Michael has four distinct roles. First, he is the Supreme Enemy of Satan and the fallen angels. He vanquished Satan and ejected him from Paradise and will achieve victory at the hour of the final battle with Satan. Secondly, he is the Christian angel of death: at the hour of death, Saint Michael descends and gives each soul the chance to redeem itself before passing. Saint Michael's third role is weighing souls in his perfectly balanced scales (hence the saint is often depicted holding scales) on Judgment Day. And finally, Saint Michael is the Guardian of the Church.[5]

I cannot find words to express the awe I will always feel whenever I consider the fact that, before I knew any of this about Saint Michael, I dreamed this dream.

> Blessed Michael, Archangel,
> defend us in the hour of conflict;
> be our safeguard against the wickedness and snares of
> the devil.
> May God restrain him, we humbly pray;
> and do thou, O Prince of the heavenly host,
> by the power of God, thrust, down to hell, Satan,
> and with him the other wicked spirits
> who wander through the world for the ruin of souls.[6]

Chapter Two – Struggles

The work is not important
only Who I honor through it
matters always and forever
God and his Son in my heart
He is why I am so driven
though my efforts seem pathetic
shed like a reptile's polished scales
my thoughts mere caterpillar's feet
chewing concepts of manifest Light
nourishing the dream of my soul
sheltered and transformed by the Word
soaring on the breath of the Holy Spirit

Indoctrination

Dream of May 1, 2011

I'm surfing hypnagogic imagery toward a white door. I can only see the strip of light at the bottom so I decide to make myself small enough to slip beneath it... Suddenly the door is wide open and my awareness instantly passes through into the dream space...

A beeping whirring sound is pursuing me, a school bus that wants to hurt me. I'm clutching a little girl's hand as we run into a white empty house, racing from room to room before taking refuge in an empty closet, where we pray the bus can't reach us...

Out on a city street with Stinger, I tell him about the bus, and confess I'm suffering from paranoid delusions. "I'm afraid God is going to begin punishing me, doling out hardships, because my life has been too easy up until now."

Sitting in a car with an excellent view of the sky to the North and West, I'm thrilled to hear an ominous rumble of thunder which I know heralds a mystical-magical event, part of a film I am watching but am also playing a part in. The northern sky flashes with a golden light expanding to reveal a colossal figure several miles high—an awful, lifeless stereotype of Jesus Christ with blind, empty eyes.

I am horribly disappointed because this is *not* what happened in the original production. All the mystery and power have been left out, and what is on display is an insipid, boring parody. I'm reminded of a depressing Ingmar Bergman film as this false Jesus speaks, droning thunderously on and on in a serious, concerned, somber voice. This utterly uninspired colossus of Christ addresses and admonishes the people of earth without any real emotion, without any love. I tell Stinger how I feel about this false man-made Christ, "I hate it!" but he disagrees, he thinks "it works." Just before waking, I see written before me very clearly: **Corinthians 1.13**.

That morning, I did a web search for "Corinthians 1:13" and could scarcely believe what I found—verses which perfectly expressed how I felt about the obviously false Christ in my dream. I had never before read this section of the New Testament. And yet, through a spiritual channel of perception opened by my dreaming mind, I was directed to these verses:

Corinthians 13.1-13
If I speak in the tongues of men and angels,
but have not love,
I have become sounding brass or a tinkling symbol.

And if I have prophecy and know all mysteries and all knowledge,
and if I have all faith so as to remove mountains,
but have not love, I am nothing.
...
Love never falls in ruins;
but whether prophecies, they will be abolished; or
tongues, they will cease; or
knowledge, it will be superseded.
...
For now we see through a mirror in an enigma, but then face to face.
Now I know in part, but then I shall know as also I was fully known.
But now remains
faith, hope, love,
these three;
but the greatest of these is love.

What I thought of in my dream as the "original production" is what truly happened when God walked among us as the Man named Jesus. I have a much better understanding now of what it means to be a Christian, as intuited by my dream—I am an active, divinely scripted player in this greatest of stories ever *still* being told and unfolding. The Holy Spirit helps direct us, through our hearts and minds, as together we work toward the supreme goal of making life "on earth as in heaven."

> "Jesus's resurrection is the beginning of God's new project not to snatch people away from earth to heaven but to colonize earth with the life of heaven. That, after all, is what the Lord's Prayer is about."[7]

Deception

Dream of May 16, 2011

I'm reclining on a bed in what looks like a nice hotel room. The darkly tanned, profoundly special man I have seen twice before in my dreams is smiling down at me. But there is something off about him; his flesh is more black than golden, and I don't experience the overwhelming love I have felt in his presence before. He tells me he has to leave for a while to attend some meetings, but all he's wearing is what looks like a white phallic sheathe, and as he begins walking away, I get a disturbing view of his bare ass cheeks.

Feeling uneasy, I remark on his state of undress, and he turns to face me again. His complacent smile broadening into a grin, he mutters something provocative as he joins me on the bed. We begin kissing, our tongues circling each others swiftly, with a feigned passion, because in truth I am immensely disappointed by the encounter, and not remotely aroused by him. Lying on my back with my legs spread, I reluctantly watch him begin slipping inside me, until I remember I haven't asked him to use protection, then I suddenly find the strength to resist him. Two or three times, I succeed in pushing him away before he finally gives up, and lays down beside me. He still looks intensely amused, and in no hurry to leave. I say, thinking out loud, "Further proof this is just a dream."

That morning I wrote: Before going to sleep last night, I prayed for a lucid dream in which I might speak with my special Guardian Lord, as I have come to think of Him. The dream character I encountered seemed to be trying to impersonate him, but he was definitely *not* Him. Every time I remember how he nearly tricked me into letting him enter me, I feel ashamed, as though I should have known better.

Years later, while reading the autobiography of Saint Theresa of Avila, I was reminded of this dream by the following passage:

> "Once more I repeat my advice that it is very important that we should not try to lift up our spirits unless they are lifted up by the Lord: in the latter case we shall become aware of the fact instantly. It is especially harmful for women to make such attempts, because the

devil can foster illusions in them, although I am convinced that the Lord never allows anyone to be harmed who strives to approach Him with humility; rather will he derive more profit and gain from the very experience through which the devil thought to send him to perdition."[8]

On that night, I had deliberately tried to dream with my special Guardian Lord, and it seems the devil strove to deceive me with the illusion of having succeeded, but I instantly knew something was wrong, because I did not feel either loved or uplifted. Theresa also says:

"Three or four times, I think, he has attempted to present the Lord Himself to me in this way, by making a false likeness of Him. He takes the form of flesh, but he cannot counterfeit the glory which the vision has when it comes from God. He makes these attempts in order to destroy the effects of the genuine vision that the soul has experienced; but the soul, of its own accord, resists them; it then becomes troubled, despondent and restless; loses the devotion and joy which it had before... And further, I think, the devil's consolations must be different from those of God; there is no suggestion in them of pure and chaste love and it very soon becomes easy to see whence they come. So, in my view, where a soul has had experience, the devil will be unable to do it any harm."[9]

The Man Upstairs

Dream of October 9, 2011

I become lucid as I remember the man upstairs who is always there above the non-stop, and usually frustrating, action of my dreams. I can feel Him up there now, waiting for me; always there and ready to receive me. Deliberately, I run away from whatever is going on in my dreams. Naked, and feeling timelessly lovely, I hurry up the steps. Just above where they curve sharply to the left, I'm not surprised—yet so *very* happy and relieved—to see Him sitting there waiting for me wearing nothing but an old pair of jeans.

I perch eagerly on his lap, slipping my arms around his neck, and He receives me willingly, lovingly, dependably, patiently. I sense a sadness in Him at the amount of time He has to spend up here without me, but I know He doesn't hold it against me; I know He is just as happy as I am that we're together now. He lifts me up a little, shifting me on His lap so that we are face to face, and I clearly see His ideally handsome features. His pale skin is clean-shaven, and His perfectly sculpted mouth, so enticingly close, returns my smile softly, in a deeply intimate way. As we kiss chastely, holding each other close, I distinctly experience the sensation of His lips. I don't remember Him sending me back downstairs, but I know I was eventually obliged to return to all the dream craziness below.

That morning I wrote: This lucid kiss filled me with a

soothing, centering calm in the midst of my chaotic dreams, and being with Him, seeing Him, experiencing the gentle intensity, the timeless familiarity of His embrace and His kiss, has given me a lift all day. I can't stop remembering those special moments above the other levels of the dream space, where I seemed to be passionately struggling with past transgressions and behavior patterns I'm striving to atone for and rise above.

◐

After this dream, I found myself wondering if I might be blessed by two special Guardian Lords, the one with the dark golden skin, and this other fair-skinned man. Of course, I knew that appearances in dreams are malleable, but it pleased me to imagine that not just one but two higher beings* loved my soul and were watching over me. (*New Age terms were my default pseudo-spiritual vocabulary at the beginning of my lucid dreaming practice.) And yet, how I felt with both these Lucid Guardians—which was how I referred to them when talking to other dreamers I felt might be put off by the term Guardian Lords—was essentially, wonderfully the same. With both of them, I basked in an unconditional love that I felt had always been there and always would be.

Vanity

Dream of October 30, 2011

I'm conscious of being myself while at the same time "inhabiting" the body and emotions of a short and somewhat stocky Hispanic woman. I can feel she is very upset about a lot of things as she walks across an open field. She–I am all fired up, filled with a passionate, righteous sense of purpose.

I detach myself from her for a moment, gazing down at her from above as I wonder how she can possibly believe she has any real influence or power over anything when she is only one of a million nondescript middle-aged women. She's not even wealthy or beautiful, and yet she's absolutely convinced of her importance, and of her power to fight the wrongs she perceives.

I slip back inside her as she–I climb a very high, steep hill. At the summit, we come upon the traditional figure of Jesus sitting on a park bench. He smiles and greets me, asking me how I am. I reply, "On the one hand, it's a good day, a *very* good day," (I am, after all, conversing with Christ!) "and yet it also sucks!"

What I mean is that even though Creation is a wonder, and everything is essentially good because it comes from God, the current state of the world is absolutely awful.

A dark-haired woman is sitting to the right of Jesus on the bench. She looks as relaxed as He does, and I can "see" into her mind—I feel/perceive that she is slightly amused by my worked up state. I know that she herself is much more lucidly aware and in control of her thoughts and emotional processes, which she gazes upon as though at the flowing eddies of a stream or the currents of a river she never allows to carry her away, much less drown her.

I don't remember if it is Jesus or his female companion who tells me about the people who climb to the top of the mountain believing that by remaining there, faithfully living and fervently waiting, a state of grace will come upon them naturally. To me it seems a silly, a ridiculous idea. And yet...

Once again slipping out of the other Hispanic woman's body and gazing down at the scene, I wonder if it is only my detached cynicism that makes the concept of Divine Grace seem childish. I wake.

I had no idea what to make of this dream, so I simply wrote it down, and moved on. I have to smile now at my own blind vanity. At the time, I didn't even realize that all the ways I described this seemingly other Hispanic woman, "short and somewhat stocky, only one of a million nondescript middle-aged women... not even wealthy or beautiful" could be applied to me, not until I read the dream again three years later, then it was painfully, laughably obvious. I may have been considered by some to have been beautiful once, but that's not the point. The point is that something inside me despised, literally looked down with contempt, at my self.

When I woke up, I was surprised I had just been talking to Christ so passionately, and yet so casually, so naturally. Not knowing what to make of it, I simply dismissed this dream as residue from my Catholic upbringing. Not for one second did I imagine my dream was precognitive, and that I was already on my way back to Christ. Yet because it appealed to my vanity, I had no problem entertaining the thought that the lovely dark-haired woman sitting beside Jesus represented my soul, and the more enlightened person I was becoming.

Reading this dream again years later was a humbling slap in the face. It forced the realization upon me that, in many respects, I am still subject to being swept away, and potentially drowned, by the destructive currents of self delusions. But now, at least, I am one of the people standing faithfully beside Christ. And if the overwhelming love, joy and gratitude I feel whenever I think about my Lord and my God is not a state of grace, I don't know what is. And this state of grace did indeed come upon me naturally, through my dreams, because I had never, deep in my heart, stopped believing in the Divine saving power of Christ's love.

Chapter Three – Dreams of Christmas

I am no longer like the mouse
weak and quivering with fear
that confronted me during yoga

Invited to attend the Wedding
by the Holy Spirit in a dream
every moment is a dance step
a continual exercise of grace
with inspired flourishes of joy
and when sadness trips me up
I hold on to my Partner
Who does all in His power
to keep us close
and never let me fall
except into His arms

A Sign

Dream of December 21, 2011—Winter Solstice

Outside at night, I somehow end up sitting at a white picnic-style table with two other women. I get the feeling we are all young. As we talk, I glance up at the sky, which is somewhat overcast, but between strips of white clouds I can just make out glimmering stars. I continue glancing up at the heavens as we converse. The moon appears to be full (*in waking reality it is a waning crescent*) which surprises and pleases me. The moon grows more and more visible, until suddenly it shoots straight down from the sky and lands on a white wall behind me. It hangs there like a three-dimensional work of art in the form of a great white fish with red fins and trims. It is a big, beautiful, plump fish approximately the width of my arms when I open them wide.

I exclaim to the women sitting at the table with me, "Look! It's the moon in the form of a fish landed on the wall!" The white fish is looking and smiling directly at me in, I feel, a teasing way, its glowing aura absolutely positive and totally lovely. It looks like a fish but I know it's really the moon, which is obviously, miraculously sentient.

I realize what is happening isn't possible, that I'm dreaming. Standing, I tell my companions, "This is a dream" careful to temper my excitement so as not to wake up. I experience the usual rush of gratitude and joy that my intent bore fruit, and I became lucid. Raising my right hand, I ask to go higher, and at once a current of force lifts and pulls me backward. I surrender to it happily, and am soon soaring straight up into the night sky.

I remember to hold my hands up before me, which helps anchor me in the dream, and to lightly touch my dream chest, but I keep these techniques to a minimum, concerned that if I think too much about my body, I'll wake up. I rise higher and higher above the ground, and the nocturnal view below me of green plains and lush forests, combined with the expansive silence all around me, is awe inspiring. Then, abruptly, I stop ascending and simply hover above the world, gazing down on it with a blissful sense of pure potential. What now? Where to go? What to do? I feel myself shifting back into waking consciousness, and soon wake.

That morning I wrote: Winter Solstice dreams are reputed to foretell events in the coming year. Despite its brevity, this dream left me with such a wonderful, positive feeling of promise. Today, I feel as I did at the end of the dream, poised on a threshold of boundless potential, ready to explore as yet unforeseen, scarcely hoped for, possibilities.

I had this dream three days before Christmas. Distracted by its luminous, delightfully mischievous beauty, I had no idea at first why the moon had taken the form of a great fish. Eventually, of course, it struck me that a fish is a symbol of Christianity.

> The Greek word for fish is "ichthys." As early as the first century, Christians made an acrostic from this word: Iesous Christos Theou Yios Soter, i.e. Jesus Christ, Son of God, Savior. The fish has plenty of other theological overtones as well, for Christ fed the 5,000 with 2 fishes and 5 loaves... and called his disciples "fishers of men." Water baptism, practiced by immersion in the early church, created a parallel between fish and converts... Greeks, Romans, and many other pagans used the fish symbol before Christians. Hence the fish, unlike, say,

the cross, attracted little suspicion, making it a perfect secret symbol for persecuted believers. When threatened by Romans in the first centuries after Christ, Christians used the fish mark... to distinguish friends from foes. According to one ancient story, when a Christian met a stranger on the road, the Christian sometimes drew one arc of the simple fish outline in the dirt. If the stranger drew the other arc, both believers knew they were in good company.[10]

I then thought about how the moon reflects the sun's light, but is in itself a dark, lifeless body... like our brains' gray matter shining as minds reflecting God's Living Light.

Teacher

Dream of December 28, 2011

An extremely attractive man with luminous blonde hair is preparing to teach a class on lucid dreaming, and I'm thrilled to be one of the group of people attending this special lecture. He steps up to the front of the class and begins speaking, instructing us to assume meditative postures. I become vividly aware then of sitting with my back against a wall. I slump slightly, resting my hands, palms facing up, on the wooden floor beside my crossed legs as I lower my head and relax.

A woman across from me informs me, her tone condescending, that I'm not doing it properly, that I haven't assumed the correct posture. Our teacher immediately tells her that I am, in fact, doing what is required. He even goes so far as to imply that my way, although different and not traditional, is just as good.

Encouraged, I relax into the posture, and the dream becomes even more exceptionally vivid, almost like being awake but much better. I feel as though I'm sitting on the deck of a ship as a strong yet gentle, perfectly temperate wind caresses me. I distinctly feel, and see, the wooden planks of the deck undulating slightly. I'm looking down at my hands, keenly observing the phenomena of some of my fingers penetrating the boards even while others rest against them, as though the deck is both substantial *and* insubstantial. It's very interesting to me that some of my fingers are able to sink into the wooden planks, while my other fingers encounter a solid resistance. I'm a bit amazed by the depth of my meditative state, and am thoroughly enjoying it —the sound and feel of the wind, the gentle rocking motion of the ship, and the play of my fingers with the magically permeable deck...

Stepping around his other students, our teacher approaches me, and I think how handsome he is, how wise and charismatic. He exudes a sublime attractive power. I can't help but be drawn to him, and I'm forced to admit to myself that this man is... hard to describe... the *ideal* man.

With words, or telepathically, I can't remember, he approves of what I'm achieving with my meditation. He then takes a moment to pull out a few discarded empty wine bottles from a crack between the deck and the wall behind me. I wasn't aware of this "trash pit" and I take a moment to shift my position, settling myself away from it...

Our teacher is standing some distance away talking to another woman in the class, and as I look up at them, a vision flashes before me of a tree with slender limbs and jade-green leaves. I somehow know they are discussing the upcoming gathering. Listening to them, I feel jealous of the people in his inner circle, and can scarcely believe it when he turns toward me and tells me that I too should come. I sense that he especially wants me there, and my happiness knows no bounds! I'm certain now that I'm not simply imagining the special interest he is taking in me. I tell him that *of course* I will come, and he instructs a woman to put my name in The Book.

The dream begins fading as I hold on to the joyful thought that our teacher seems to want me near him as much as I want to be around him. When I wake completely, I suffer a sinking disappointment, bordering on despair, that it was all just a dream.

I had the Moon Fish dream three days before Christmas, and this dream three days after Christmas. It seems incredible to me now that I didn't understand what was happening. I could not see the forest for the trees.

My joy in the dream, when our teacher commanded my name be written in The Book, was equaled only by my sinking disappointment when I woke up, and lost sight of Him. I had heard of the Book of Life, but never investigated its origins. I longed to understand who these Guardian Lords were. Even though they could vary slightly or even dramatically in appearance, they always made me feel the same way—irresistibly drawn to them, and nearly overwhelmed with happiness by the attention they paid me.

In the process of writing this book, I finally Googled "Christianity Book of Life" and received an education:

> The term "The Book of Life" appears in both the Old Testament and New Testament. In the Psalms, those who are obedient to God among the living are considered worthy of having their name entered in The Book. Jesus Christ alludes to the Book of Life in Luke 10:20, when he tells the seventy disciples to rejoice because "your names are written in heaven." Paul says the names of his fellow missionary workers "are in the Book of Life." Believers in Christ are assured that their names are recorded in the Lamb's Book of Life and that they have nothing to fear as He keeps and protects them during their earthly journey.[11]

In my dream—on the deck of a ship that was both physical and transcendent—our wise and beautiful teacher was instructing us in lucid dreaming as a spiritual exercise. I had been lucid dreaming on a consistent basis for nearly a year now, and it was already transforming my life. I had begun healing myself in dreams, both emotionally and physically, but I also knew I was only at the very beginning of my journey. In this dream, my teacher discarded some empty wine bottles I had been leaning against, thereby gently making it clear to me that I should clean up my act. Almost overnight, I went from drinking nearly an entire bottle of wine every evening to just one or two glasses of wine with dinner. I didn't force myself to do it; the craving, the need to drink more in order to relax and feel good, was simply gone.

My first lucid dreaming related article *Mirror Mirror on the Wall: Lucid Dreaming and Menopause* had just been published in the *Lucid Dream Exchange* (Winter Edition, Number 61, December 2011.) My experience with healing my tendinitis[12] in a series of lucid dreams was published six months later in the *Lucid Dream Exchange* (Vol. 1, No. 1, June 2012.) I include below an abridged version of this article, because it puts the dreams I was having with my special Guardian Lords into the context of my developing lucid dreaming practice, and how it was changing what I believed to be possible.

Healing My Tendinitis in Lucid Dreams

> As a writer, visual artist, and passionate cook, I spend a lot of time typing, using a mouse, and chopping ingredients, activities that all make rather excessive use of my right hand, thumb, wrist and arm. In fact, I relied almost exclusively on the right side of my body until the day I tripped and fell while playing catch-the-stick with my puppy. I broke my fall with both hands and

thought nothing of it, until a few days later, when it became excruciatingly apparent something was terribly wrong with my right wrist and thumb. The pain when I moved them in certain directions was so intense, I was forced to begin using my left hand for whatever tasks I could manage to accomplish with it. I bought a cloth brace and began wearing it night and day, hoping that whatever was wrong would get better, but days and then weeks passed with no sign of improvement. I continued to type and use a mouse, cook and do yoga, yet the range of motion in my wrist and thumb was limited by instant and severe pain. Desiring to avoid a cortisone shot at all cost, I tried two weeks of electrical heat stimulation, ultrasounds, massages and physical therapy with a chiropractor. After the treatment ended, I continued doing the stretches they had taught me at home, but my condition showed no real improvement.

I did not immediately attempt to heal myself in a lucid dream because I felt I was suffering from a life-style injury that was teaching me important lessons about balancing both sides of my self, in every sense. I didn't feel it was right to want to fix a non life-threatening condition which was helping me grow. On the other hand, the constant inconvenience of a brace—and the occasional excruciating pain when it failed to keep my wrist and/or thumb from moving in a certain direction—was really getting old. There was also the concern that my tendinitis (for so the chiropractor diagnosed it) if not dealt with in a timely fashion might become chronic. Therefore, before scheduling the dreaded cortisone shot, I consciously stepped past the mental and emotional assumptions causing me to treat the power behind the dream like a genie granting me only three big wishes I should be afraid of wasting. I decided to try to heal myself in a lucid dream.

Dream of September 2011
I find myself fully conscious of being awake in a dream where I'm lying on my back on my bed in our bedroom, which is dark. I raise my right hand toward the ceiling thinking *make light* and violet sparkles emanate from my fingertips which delight me, and also succeed in gently illuminating the ceiling, where a circular decorative carving has replaced our actual ceiling fan. I notice then that my right hand is wearing the cloth brace I've been subjected to for weeks now because of a strained tendon. (Yesterday it was worse than ever; I couldn't move my thumb in any direction without pain shooting through me, so that I was obliged to skip yoga, which really upset me.)

At once, I remember my intent. Raising both hands before me, I point the index finger of my left hand at the junction of my right wrist and thumb, willing a healing energy into it. I'm delighted to see a stream of lovely blue and violet sparkles (I can't think of a better word for them.) I then take the time to remove the cloth brace so it won't be in the way, and direct the starry healing energy to just above the tender area. At one point I can't see anything, but I'm aware of lying in bed having this lucid dream, and of struggling to disconnect the desire to open my eyes in the dream with the urge to open my actual physical eyes, which will wake me up.

I don't know how I manage it, perhaps through sheer willpower, but I find myself once again gazing at the dream room and my hands. I turn my right hand, so I can see the bottom of my wrist, and trace my left index finger along it. I can see beneath the skin; a section of skin seems to be missing. I discern a black line or band of sorts which at first looks like an inverted syringe with something sharp and dark moving up my arm from my wrist. I'm quite fascinated to be seeing the inside of my body as I continue directing healing energy into it that consists of a shimmering violet light indistinguishable from my intent, which is the real mysterious source of the "corrective" power I'm focusing on my wrist and thumb. I become aware of a golden light slightly behind me to my left and give thanks for this dream as it slowly fades and I find myself awake in bed.

At once I told my husband about the dream, and removing the cloth brace declared with complete faith, "Look!" as I moved my wrist and thumb around in different directions without much pain. "It's still not one-hundred percent, but it's *much* better! And morning is when it hurts the most! I wish I'd had more time!"

If I have to assign a percentage to the improvement in my condition, I would say seventy-five percent. My wrist also feels *so* much stronger, nowhere near as weak and vulnerable to being accidentally moved in the wrong direction. It's very interesting how connected I feel to this part of my body after seeing it in the dream, and seeing *into* it. I look at it now and feel as though I can will it to get better, that my intent is still connected to it in an active way.

I've become aware of all my hand motions these past few weeks, but this morning I feel reverently connected to my right hand and wrist in a way I never have before. As always happens with a lucid dream, I *feel* differently about something, not just *think* differently.

Dream of November 2011
...I begin walking down a corridor and, looking down at my wrist, I move it around and don't feel any discomfort or tightness. I think that when I wake up, my wrist will feel just like it does here in my dream body. I turn around and start walking back the way I came. Then, standing against a wall, I recite, "I'm radiant with health, I'm radiant with health" and begin walking again.

I raise my hands slightly before me, and visualize blue

healing energy coming out of my left index finger toward the problem spot in my right wrist. I'm gratified to see it, and by how effortless it is. Then I decide to make the healing energy more direct and intense, like a laser, and it transforms into a violet shaft of solid light that darkens to a shimmering purple. I look for my tendon to make sure I'm directing the energy into the right place, and gradually begin waking up.

This morning, I've been able to stretch and move my wrist and thumb even more freely than before just by remembering what my dream body felt like, and by visualizing the tendon as I saw it in the dream. I'm concentrating on my thumb's mobility now, and on fully opening my hand as I haven't been able to do in weeks.

In conclusion, I appear to have reduced the inflammation in my wrist in lucid dreaming equivalents of cortisone shots. Each time after I woke up, I moved and stretched my thumb and wrist in ways I couldn't before, and I repeated these exercises several times during the day, feeling I was helping align my physical body with my dream body so its healing energy could be more effectively absorbed.

My tendinitis soon disappeared completely, and after more than three years has not returned.

Glass Bus

Dream of January 20, 2012

I'm sitting on a bus at night. I have no clue I'm dreaming; it feels quite real being on a bus riding through a city, a poorer section, not dangerous but not the best place to work either, which is vaguely why I'm here. It's dark inside the bus as well as outside, where I can just make out white sidewalks.

As the bus makes a right turn and swiftly begins accelerating, I suddenly realize my stop is coming up. I see the push bar just ahead of me on the right, but I know I won't be able to reach it in time. I cry, "Please stop the bus! I can't reach the chord, my arm is stiff!" I'm a little surprised, and very glad, when the driver brakes, managing to stop just in time even though the bus was moving very fast. I watch myself get off the bus, even as I also remain on the bus. Observing the me standing out on the sidewalk, I think she should stay there for a few moments, with one of her arms held stiffly at her side, so the bus driver won't suspect I lied to him. But I immediately discard the thought as dishonest and unnecessary. The me on the bus is relieved for the me who needed to get off, and glad the process went smoothly. There are no other passengers. The driver is invisible in the darkness, but I sense his presence.

The bus moves on and begins accelerating faster and faster through the night. The reckless speed should alarm me, but instead it intrigues me. The driver's confidence, his unrelenting drive, pleases me; it feels good. Then suddenly the roof of the bus is transparent, and just above it, in a sunlit blue sky, I see what looks like a sleek military plane, one of the fastest planes in existence, and not only are we swiftly gaining on it, we're passing it... I must be dreaming!

I'm very happy to realize I'm in a dream even though I can't see a thing now. Darkness, and the sense of moving forward at a great speed, adds up to a sense of peace and contentment. I have no idea where we're headed; the concern doesn't really even cross my mind. I'm here and I'm going, and being here is the same as being there, the same as traveling.

When my visuals return, I can see straight through the bus, which is now floating in the sky so high above the ground, I no longer have any sense of the world being there, nor do I care. There is no coherent sense of up and down in this soft white sky, in which I suddenly see the upper body of a perfect man rendered in soft black lines. His colossal head, shoulders and naked torso are the size of a mountain peak slowly turning toward me.

I think—In a moment I'm going to see His face, the face of God. And yet I know that any man's face I see will be the face of God, for God is in all men. But I only see a fraction of His face before He stops turning toward me.

I sit there expectantly, eagerly waiting to embrace Him, to join with Him, even though I am small and confined while He is one with the endless sky. When after a long moment nothing happens, I reach up, longing to caress his bare chest, to *feel* Him. When instead I encounter a glass ceiling, I cry, "What's this?" slapping my hands in frustration against an invisible barrier that shouldn't be there, but distinctly is.

I lower my hands and become aware that beneath my shirt, my bra is slipping down over my nipples, making me very conscious of my breasts in an arousing way. I feel a swelling tide of sexual desire, but instead of riding it like a surfer catching a wave, which I know will only land me back in bed, I let it flow past me. The transparent bus is still moving forward as I slowly wake.

> Jesus said in John 14:9, "If you have seen me you have seen the Father."... Jesus was the physical representation of God the Father, and although when we see Him we see God, we do not see the full and total manifestation of the Father. That is, we do not see the Father in His full glory (otherwise we would die). This is captured in John 1:18 when John says that "no one has seen God at any time." Jesus, although God, was "limited" or "subjected" by the flesh... Revelation 22:4 is a very special verse: **"They will see the face of God."** It is the culmination of the revelation of God. Scholars deem it "The Beatific Vision." To "see the face of God" will be an incredible moment and experience, and it is not unreasonable to suggest that this is more than what man has experienced in the past... It is first important to understand the context of Revelation 22:4. This experience will take place in the New Heaven and New Earth. This means that the verse is for believers, and that the believers will be in their resurrected bodies.

Paul calls this "the change" (1 Corinthians 15:50-58). ...Man in his former state cannot look upon the face of God and live... When man is finally able to "see the face of God" it will indeed be an incredible moment. This is because man will finally experience the fullness of God.[13]

Thy true face is freed from any limitation, it hath neither quantity nor quality, nor is it of time or place, for it is the Absolute Form, the Face of faces... For all concept of a face falleth short, Lord, of Thy face, and all beauty that can be conceived is less than the beauty of Thy face; every face hath beauty yet none is beauty's self, but Thy face, Lord, hath beauty and this having is being. 'Tis therefore Absolute Beauty itself, which is the form that giveth being to every beautiful form.[14]

A Prayer

Dream of March 28, 2012

Lots of dreams last night, but there was one particularly vivid section involving a man and a woman who had done something rebellious, and left a notice posted in a small Virginia town, defying convention, ahead of their time. The note was full of passion and an ironic, impatient attitude toward social hypocrisy.

Suddenly, my dreaming awareness is "zooming" in on the woman, on who she is and when she lived. "Squinting" my consciousness, making an intent effort to focus, I distinctly make out the date: **1880**. This means she's dead now, which is disappointing. I then, very clearly, receive the name of the place where she is buried, as I both see it written and hear it spoken: **Buckeye Cemetery**.

Now I'm in a dark shop, old-fashioned in feel and appearance, with lots of small, colorful items, perhaps for sewing and embroidering. I see an old woman perched on a stool, and at the same time I *am* her. She-we are sitting in the center of the space, and we want to remain there, child-like, where we can look around at all the pretty things, at all the colorful possibilities... but she is at death's door... she is dead now...

The next day, I wrote: I ignored this dream all morning, thinking it was silly, that there would be no such thing as a Buckeye cemetery, but then I did a web search and discovered there's a whole area called Buckeye in West Virginia, and an actual Buckeye Cemetery. I found a website with a photo of all the graves there, and only one of them showed a birth date of 1880: **Susie S. Mayo 1880-1950**. Written on her gravestone are the words:

LOVE LIGHT MY WAY TO GOD

She was an older woman when she died, as I perceived in my dream. I also found a notice in a local newspaper mentioning that so-and-so and Miss Susie Mayo were expecting two guests for Christmas on December 21, 1946, two men.

I feel that, for some reason I cannot fathom, Susie wanted me to read what she chose to write on her grave marker. I feel she gave me the gift of a personal mantra that truly resonates with me: LOVE LIGHT MY WAY TO GOD, a prayer that will help light my way for the rest of my life. I don't feel the dream's intent was to urge me to look up more information about her. When I recite her epitaph, out loud or in my mind, especially when I'm outside facing the sun, I'm suffused by a powerful sense of well being. Thank you, Susie.

Chapter Four – The Lord is With Us

Much as I love a deep tissue massage
it is just another fleeting pleasure compared
to the joy of loving God with every breath
and beat of my miraculous little heart.
This body will soon be tossed aside
like clothing on a wedding night
everything made and unmade by Him
for His pleasure which is all I am
and desire to be an expression of Love.
All I see and know is His Spirit
my miserable self is only happy striving
to be as beautiful as possible for Him
impatiently discarding ragged reason
and the clinging filth of doubts and fears
I joyfully weave my thoughts and feelings
into the service of this love and longing
for the Lord of Life and Master of death
Eternity His gift for my devotion to Us.

Triptych

Dreams of May 2, 2012

#1 – I arrive in a city in the company of another woman I rescued from working for a corrupt Chinese company. I lead the woman into a building, and we ascend to the top floor. Guarding the entrance, a row of uniformed men are standing just outside the suite where He is waiting for us. I salute them all with a flourish, and my mockingly intense precision makes one of them laugh. I enter the spacious room feeling a little apologetic about being here again so soon as I say to Him, "You can't get any peace" but He welcomes me with open arms, a loving, almost eager expression on his face that silently commands, "Come here."

I happily slip my arms around his neck. He is a tall, handsome blonde man casually but elegantly clad in a white dress shirt and dark slacks, and resting in the shelter of his embrace is pure, absolute happiness. I lean against his left side so that my companion can also embrace him. I have brought her to Him so He can help her. There is no question of being jealous, for he is wonderful enough for both of us, marvelous enough for everyone!

#2 – Christ is sitting in my bathroom with a little boy who is my brother, even though in reality he is a grown man. I enter the bathroom and, needing to relieve myself, sit down on the toilet. I say something about it being interesting, and very cool, that we're preparing to combine a spiritual exercise with the exercise of our "gross" bodily functions; that there is a good balance in this.

I sense Christ helping my brother to focus his mind so that together they can generate light. I comment on how bright my nightlight is which in the dream is plugged in where the toilet paper is in reality. Christ tells me that I will never get it done (the spiritual exercise) with the nightlight on, which makes perfect sense, so I turn it off, or it simply turns off by itself. We are now plunged into total darkness, and I'm very glad of this because the darkness feels good, full of potential, holy with Christ's presence. Now the exercise of generating light from within us can truly begin.

#3 – I'm witnessing, and am also accompanying, a family making a difficult escape on the edge of a turbulent ocean. We are fleeing the evil pursuing us, but have paused to rest on top of a large rock, where we discuss strategy. One man, who is holding a male child, insists the plan has to be simple, because he's not certain he can keep the child safe through any complex situations.

Another man, the one leading us, responds with single words, "Ocean. Command. Plan. Formed. In effect."

Somehow grasping what he means, I exclaim, "I love it when he talks that way!" I know he has full command over the ocean, and can navigate all dangers and threats we encounter on our journey. The important thing is not to linger doubtfully, afraid of not being able to handle whatever awaits us, for he is with us and will protect and guide us.

Because I continue to read my leaders, and so have been blessed with discovering the books of N.T. Wright, I can now discern that these three dreams shared a common theme—how God is present and active in His creation through Jesus Christ, the Son of Man, whose breath is the Holy Spirit.

Regarding my third and final dream: The rock on which we rested in the midst of our deliverance from evil, I now interpret as representing Christianity. The man clinging protectively to the male child symbolizes Christians who, not fully understanding Jesus, seek to shelter him, and themselves, from any dangerous involvement with worldly powers, fearing that His message is too naive, too innocent to stand up to them. They do not realize that Christ is already, in Truth, the one and only Lord of the world—the Man in my dream who was guiding and protecting us, the Man I knew could command the ocean and all other destructive forces, the Man who made it clear that a fully formed plan is in effect—God's plan to save us.

In my second dream, Jesus was teaching my brother and I how to generate light from within us. Christ was sitting with us in a dark bathroom, technically not a sacred space, but the fact is that when Jesus rose from the dead, He did not leave his corpse behind in the tomb—His actual physical body was resurrected. One of the reasons I became estranged from Christianity as a young woman was the mistaken idea that my sensuality and my spirituality were eternally opposed to each other, and that making it into heaven demanded I forever surrender all my senses and desires. Pope John Paul II wrote:

> Far from condemning the body, Christ calls the total person to purity. True Christian morality doesn't flee bodily existence—it embraces and sanctifies it... The body shares in our dignity as persons, just as much as the spirit. The body manifests the spirit... Though man

is sinful, this doesn't mean the body is evil... Anyone who reads a negative view of the body and sexuality into Christ's teaching makes a fundamental error... The right Christian attitude aims at purifying the heart so we can see the true value of the body... God created us by grace, and he can redeem us by grace...We are called to love. We are called to live the truth of our bodies, in their masculinity and femininity. This is our heritage from the beginning, the heritage of the heart, which goes far deeper than lust... Through Christ's redeeming grace, the heart's fundamental longing for love is affirmed and empowered... Christ seeks to redeem what has been weighed down by sin... Passion (eros) and purity (ethos) are not opposed to one another. Instead, they are called to meet and bear fruit in the human heart.[15]

In my first dream, I was acting as a good citizen of Christ's kingdom, guiding a suffering soul into His loving embrace. Angels in the form of police officers guarded the doors of heaven, which took the form of the top floor of a highrise building on earth. As a lucid dreamer, I already feel I have two bodies in one—my physical body and my dream body, which technically occupy the same space, but do not share the same limitations.

> "...It will not do to suppose that Jesus came to teach people 'how to get to heaven.' That view has been immensely popular in western Christianity for many

generations, but it simply won't do. The whole point of Jesus' public career was not to tell people that God was in heaven and that, at death, they could leave 'earth' behind and go to be with him there. It was to tell them that God was now taking charge, right here on 'earth'; that they should recognize, in his own work, the signs that it was happening indeed; and that when he completed his work, it would become reality."[16]

Waiting and Wanting

Dream of May 12, 2012

I don't remember exactly what was happening as I became lucid, but it was a slow, seamless transition; I sort of willed it. I think I sensed my sleeping body, and that it might wake up at any moment, and thought—No, I'm going to keep going in this dream. I made myself lucid, and from the start I was so well grounded in the dream, I hardly bothered with deepening or sustaining techniques.

Fully lucid, I'm walking through a plain, empty room toward a large window. I extend my hands toward it, intending to go through it, but instead I simply peel it off, like a large piece of very thin stiff plastic which offers no resistance. I step outside, onto an empty city street at dusk, and begin rising up into an overcast sky. I can't see the moon, so I'm unable to fulfill my intent of plucking it out of the sky, and swallowing it like a glowing pill of perfect health and well-being. Well, it doesn't matter, and suddenly I'm surprised by a very real sensation of warmth emanating from the dream space ahead of me. I'm flying toward it, very conscious of the fact that it's very strange, very special for me to experience a distinct feeling of warmth in a dream.

As my dream body drifts eastward, I find myself flying close to the ground above some kind of garden party. Below me, little girls and young women are strolling, all of them wearing long white dresses. Gliding almost parallel to the ground, I gaze curiously down at the gathering as I gently gain altitude. One little girl is aware of me, and we keep looking at each other, but I'm still surprised when she reaches up toward me, and then actually leaves the ground. Smiling, I grasp her hand, and she joins me in my leisurely cruise through the air. She is not only wearing white, she herself is entirely white (*or so I remember her*) like a ghost, but perfectly solid.

Her old-fashioned dress inspires me to ask her, "Where is this? What *year* is this?"

Replying slowly, as though she can't quite understand the question because the answer is obvious, she says, "This is the year that God made."

Enchanted by her response, I declare, "Well, that's the best year ever, isn't it!"

I become aware that several other figures are now floating around us, individuals of all ages, including an infant and a very old woman. When a man wearing an old-fashioned suit that strikes me as Victorian comes very close to me, I ask him, "Where is this place?" and he tells me, "This is the Mea Culpa gathering."

Abruptly, I somehow understand these people are all dead and waiting here for something, for *someone*. In a flash, I see a vision of a luminous, healing Being of Light my heart recognizes as Christ, and I understand that while these people wait, they are atoning for some major sin or sins for which they (rightly?) blame themselves. I'm surprised even supposedly innocent babies find themselves here. But the man is "flying" a little too close to me, almost as though he wants to look up my skirt, and I decide it's time to move on.

No sooner do I separate myself from the floating, drifting people, that I find myself walking through a large house, which is ostensibly still part of the Mea Culpa gathering. I stride determinedly down a narrow corridor, which I sense leads to the rear of the building, searching for a back door. I find one in a small narrow kitchen, where a woman is standing at the stove cooking and pays me no heed. The door opens inward. Shoving two trash cans gently out of the way, I think with satisfaction—There's *always* a back door.

I step out into what I can only describe as a patio-annex crowded with wooden furniture, knickknacks and window blinds. I lift them out of my way as I step carefully over the barrier, only slightly disturbing one or two objects while thinking—I'd better be careful not to damage anything or I might end up in one of these Mea Culpa gatherings. Wow, I actually made a joke in a lucid dream...

I find myself outside at night in a stark black-and-white city, in a warehouse-like district, where the buildings appear constructed of porous old concrete. There are no street lights, and no people; the city looks completely deserted. Walking down a sidewalk even though there aren't any cars, I cry out to my Guardian Lord, "I love you! I love you! And one night, I hope to see you and to talk to you again in a dream!"

I sink to my knees and clasp my hands before me, showing him how much I respect Him, and how thankful I am for His presence in my dreams as I repeat, "I love you!"

Suddenly, streaming across the black sky, I perceive a series of banner-like rectangles, each one framing glimmering, silver-white words written in a clean print font, as though typed in starlight. The banners are not attached to any kind of plane as they fly swiftly over me, and I can just barely read the three words they contain: **I Am Here**.

As I continue looking up at the banners soaring by overhead, I'm almost positive that's what they say, but I can't be absolutely sure, and the more of an effort I make to read them, the less I am able to do so.

Belatedly, I fly onto a roof top to get a closer look, at which point two or three of the banners fly back toward me. I'm able to grab hold of one, and as I do so, it transforms into a clear shining pouch containing lovely white lingerie, delicate bras and panties made of a pure, glittering, luminous material. I'm so surprised, I can't make any sense of it. It almost seems like my Guardian Lord is teasing me? I phase out of the dream.

The end of this incredible night of lucid dreaming caused me such a sweet pain! On the one hand, the starry lingerie seemed an obvious promise from my Guardian Lord of greater intimacy to come, yet a part of me worried it might also be a warning that there would always be an invisible barrier between us for as long as I felt attracted to him the way a woman is to a man. But that didn't really make sense because the beautiful lingerie, shimmering as if stitched with starlight, had felt like a gift, not a threat, like a promise, not a reprimand. Frustration and confusion mixed with awe and hope only served to stoke and intensify my longing for Him, whoever *He* was.

> Then Jesus told her, "The I AM is here." John 4:26 [17]

> "You have often heard that God spiritually espouses souls; may He be praised for His mercy in thus humbling Himself so utterly... The soul makes amorous complaints to its Bridegroom, even uttering them aloud; nor can it control itself, knowing that though He is present He will not manifest Himself so that it may enjoy Him. This causes a pain keenly, although sweet and delicious, from which the soul could not escape even if it wished; but this it never desires." [18]

Rescued

Dream of May 27, 2012

Absolutely delighted to be lucid in a dream, I soar out of the room and fly low through the sky. Almost immediately, I come upon a large mirror with a gilded frame, in which I see myself reflected as I look now in waking reality. I'm wearing the dress I actually wore that evening before bed, and the only difference is that my skin is black!

Moving closer to the mirror, I study my complexion, and determine that it's not paint, or ashes, or any other external substance, for I am able to distinguish the natural pores in my skin. I smile at myself, intrigued to see what I might have looked like as a black woman. Flying around the left side of the mirror, I end up in front of a long, tall, perfectly white wall which, for some reason, I feel compelled to climb up rather than fly over.

I'm no longer alone; several other women are standing in this narrow corridor created by two pure white walls. The women are all attractive, and dressed in form-fitting outfits of various colors. At first we ignore each other, intent on struggling to scale the walls. Wondering why we can't just fly over them, I promptly do just that. A few of the women follow me, and one of them unexpectedly attacks me, biting the right side of my neck. Shoving her away, I'm somehow able to prevent her from coming any closer. I can scarcely believe it when she complains to the other women about my aggressive behavior. "Are you kidding?" I demand. "*You're* the one who bit *my* neck!"

Anxious to leave there, I fly Superman style straight up toward the ceiling, intending to pass through it. I penetrate it easily, but then abruptly have no desire to make the effort required to traverse this white matter, which is like no earthly material I am familiar with. The pure white substance is both a solid and a liquid, densely resistant, yet no more substantial than fog. I don't feel like struggling with it and so reverse my direction, but the ceiling follows me down, collapsing around me. This has never happened to me before in a lucid dream, but there is no getting away from it. I'm pushed down, engulfed in the whiteness pinning me beneath it. I've also never had a lucid dream end on a negative note, and I have no intention of waking up. I stop fighting the substance in which I'm trapped, and instead attempt to transform it into pure potential. I visualize the infinite whiteness as separate points of light comparable to all the stars in every possible universe. As I will myself into the light, a faint golden glow begins suffusing my white prison...

Suddenly, I am whisked away from there, carried off by a force cradling me from behind and propelling me forward at the speed of light, that's the only way I can describe it. Not far below me, I glimpse a golden light that takes the form of electricity illuminating what appears to be a cafe with glass walls reminiscent of the painting *Night Owls*. Then a Voice distinctly tells me, "You can have anything you want." This Voice is a Presence, and what it says rings with the truth of revelation.

It is nearly impossible to put into words the intensity and depth of what I experienced rescued and embraced by this Force propelling me forward, and then settling me safely inside the luminous cafe, at a small round table, while explaining to me, "It can never be defined, the mistake is to try, because if It could be so contained, It would not be what It is." I'm not being told something I haven't already conceived of intellectually, but now the truth of the words feels branded into my soul by this Voice.

That morning I wrote: The Voice did not come from within me. It felt "other", outside of me, as though it was one with the dream space itself. I myself did not "speak" the words; they did not emanate from my mind. I felt embraced, in every sense, and everything the Voice said to me was part of this embrace. I was not embracing or talking to myself; I was being embraced and spoken to, and this all happened in my soul.

> "It will be well, I think, to explain the nature of the locutions which God bestows upon the soul... Though perfectly formed, the words are not heard with the bodily ear; yet they are understood much more clearly than if they were so heard."[19]

Countless people report having heard a disembodied Voice in their dreams that speaks to them with a mysterious, undeniable authority. Carl Jung wrote:

> The 'Voice' is always a matter of an authoritative declaration or command, either of astonishing common sense and truth, or of profound philosophic allusion... It is nearly always a definite statement, usually toward the end of a dream, and it is, as a rule, so clear and convincing that the dreamer finds no argument against it.[20]

I personally feel there is only one Voice, and agree with Jung as to its Divine source. For me, the Voice is a Presence that is always there within me because I live in God as one of His created and beloved souls. I feel the Voice is the Holy Spirit, Who breathes life into our soul, and Who speaks to us in a myriad of ways to aid us on our spiritual journey toward full union with God. I feel this dream Voice is just one manifestation of the love and attention God devotes to every soul.

Purification

Dream of August 23, 2012

I'm in my bedroom floating face down a few feet above the floor, my limbs and head hanging down perfectly relaxed. I am lucidly conscious of the fact that my heart is being worked on, cleansed, purified of past transgressions. I can feel it, in the sense of actually seeing the circle over my heart, which is a luminous red-orange color and *alive*. It isn't so much an opening as an energy center, and it is spinning around and around even though it doesn't really move like that.

There is a young woman sitting to my left observing, and reading from a book. At one point, I tilt slightly to the left, but simply by willing it, without any apparent effort, straighten myself out again. I'm so happy to be undergoing what I can feel is a successful purification. Finally, I land gently on my right side, and as the young woman curiously inspects the area over my heart, she says, "There's nothing there." I explain to her that the effects aren't visible to the eye because they aren't physical. The change happened inside me, in my heart.

Chapter Five – Communicating

I treasure and preserve
this fragile envelope of flesh
for through it is delivered
the letter of God's Love
for me and all of Us

Is this why as I grow older
my skin resembles parchment
thinning and drying under the sun
to remind me the ink of my blood
means nothing without a Divine Author?

In every one the script of a unique identity
my cells rush along transmission lines
reproducing creating killing and dying
all possible histories alive within me

The ink of my life warmly flowing
my Lord communicates in every moment
joints cracking the scratch of His pen
composing another love story through one
who for so long resisted His courtship
believing Him too good to be true
and fearing to lose her desires in Him
she ran off with arrogant devils instead
her vanity stroked by too many men
who cared little for her soul's beauty

Not until her restless drives slowed down
and her pride crashed with mirrors
did she finally turn off the world's chatter
step out of an automatic self obsession
and flee the traffic jam of reason and religions
burning the finite dead fuel of the mind
to focus her vision on the living Spirit
the Light and Life knocking with her heartbeats
on the door of her dreams opening to the One
Who loves her and she loves above all things

There can never be enough worlds and words
to please and exalt my Creator-Savior-Lover

The Kiss

Dream of September 17, 2012

I'm in a vast room, part of a seemingly endless structure of dark gray stone. I'm propelling myself from one massive ledge to another, bridging the gap between them with a staff-like metal adze. I hear the sound of someone plummeting down through the dark narrow space between two of these giant stones... Or is this person ascending, rising against gravity?

The dream becomes sharp and present, semi-lucid, as I lay on my side across one of these stones. Then, as if I have always been there, I find myself reclining on a great bed. I'm wearing a long green gown, and am conscious of being another woman, and yet also myself, as I hear a quietly thunderous rushing sound emanating from within the ceiling directly across from me.

Traveling through the darkness and landing lightly, effortlessly, the man I love appears abruptly, wearing a long hooded robe of a deep, royal, gorgeous blue. The woman I am in the dream recognizes Him in the deepest sense, and hopes He has come because He knows I have been waiting for him, and that I long to do anything I can to help Him, anything He asks of me.

Before I know it, He has joined me on the bed, and is cradling me in his arms. Gazing up at his face, I whisper, "I scarcely feel worthy..." of Him, of His love.

Framed by a dark and neatly trimmed beard, His gently smiling mouth does not move as He responds, "You will simply have to get used to it."

The suspense is exquisite as our lips draw closer, and when He kisses me, the moment contains everything I wish for even as I wake up.

That morning I wrote: It is almost impossible to describe how this dream has made me feel, full of joy and longing in equal measure. I feel my soul lived that kiss, but my poor little brain cannot possibly remember and contain the depth of the experience. I sent Mami the dream, and she told me that, for Christian mystics, the union of the soul with God is called the Kiss of the Spouse, and that a kiss is symbolic of touching souls and exchanging inner worlds.

Dream Sharing

Not long after this dream, I began corresponding with another lucid dreamer on the online forum *Mortal Mist*. James Kroll and I were both extremely interested in exploring the possibility of consciously meeting in the dream space, and we soon began attempting to experience a shared lucid dream, targeting specific nights when we would intend to become lucid and meet up in what he termed mind-space. We saw this as a wonderfully original challenge, with profound implications, and completely believed it was possible.

We pursued our weekly experiments for nearly a year, and the results clearly indicate that transcending the constraints of time and space is a natural ability of consciousness.

We never met physically in waking reality, but a dream link between us could be consistently created with intent, with dream imagery being shared, even "bounced" back and forth, over the course of the night and ongoing nights. It was also possible for us to have a mutual lucid dream with a remarkable level of cognitive recovery and shared dream images.

James and I presented our findings at the 2013 International Association For the Study of Dreams Psiber Conference. In our Presentation, we briefly summarized a full year of our experiences, documenting our strategies, and the dynamic approach we used to better negotiate the dream space individually and together.[21]

Because I met James Kroll soon after my dream **The Kiss**, I initially assumed he was the man I had been waiting for, and that the kiss symbolized our souls meeting in the dream space. I became so involved in our dream sharing partnership that I was able to ignore how disappointed I was by this interpretation, because James—like no other mortal—ever made me feel remotely like the Man in royal blue robes had.

There is no doubt in my mind now that James was *not* the man whose kiss felt like closing the eyes of my brain, and diving into the depths of my soul. Yet it does seem to me that one of the promises and gifts I received through that kiss was the path I would soon embark upon—the exploration of dream sharing. In 2014, I once again presented on the subject at the IASD Psiber Dream Conference with a paper entitled, *Beyond Time and Space: The Transcendent Nature of Dream Sharing*. Below are two excerpts from this Presentation, which feature three of my dream partners—Sean, his then nine-year-old daughter, Illeana, and Igor:

Dream Share of January 26, 2014: Meeting at the Tree

Igor: Fell asleep very fast... I looked around and created a huge field with grass and one large tree... I summoned only those who wished to share a dream...

Sean: I head toward the tree. "ILLEANA!" I call out to her. I look around and see fields... I hear her cry, "I'm over here daddy!" I fly over to her. She is one-hundred percent Illeana... I look around for the tree, but as usual I'm confused... it starts off that I think I have the right tree, but it changes and I'm just not sure.

Illeana. I head toward the tree and see Daddy coming to the tree at the same time. When he arrives he looks a little confused. I shout at him and shake him, "DADDY!" He seems to snap into it and is "really" with me now.

Sean. "Can you see the tree Illy?" She takes about two seconds scanning the countryside. "There it is." She points directly to it and, sure enough, that is the tree! "Let's fast travel there," I say to her. She replies, "Yeah, like in Minecraft." We zoom there, focusing on the tree and bringing it to us.

Maria. I will myself to quantum jump from here to the tree instead of just flying. I impulsively try this new "quantum leap" method a few times without results, at which point I begin rising up into the sky...

Illeana. The tree is like it is in real life, not how I built it.

Sean. The tree is magnificent, it is SO clear. It looks like it is in real life, though it is taller than usual. I see the makeshift swing hanging from its branch. I'm about to land next to it when I spot a very strange sight—a man sitting or standing high up on a branch of the tree...

Maria: I'm flying high above beautiful bright countryside. Very soon I see a magnificent tree, so large and tall that its highest branches are almost level with me. A man is standing on one of the upper branches. I fly purposefully toward him, grab the branch, and swing the final distance to him. Abruptly I'm facing what appear to be three people. Only one of them is distinct and speaks, but doesn't seem to hear me...

Sean: We land next to the tree. I say to Illy, "We will go see Igor then Maria."

Illeana: Dad says to me, "We will go see Igor then Maria." I nod, and we make a portal together. We step through into the void. Igor is there... we cannot hear what he says back to me. We then make another Portal and see Maria... She talks, but we can't hear her.

Dream Share of February 23, 2014: Dream Walking

Maria: In some sweet spot between a WILD[22] and a DILD[23], I'm suddenly standing in white space beside a man dressed in black. He's holding my right hand as though he pulled me there, or as if I pulled him there. I look at his face, which is very close, and say, "Igor?" Our eyes meet, slide away as though against some invisible force field, then meet again. I repeat, "Is it you, Igor?" His smile, absolute presence, and sentient eyes all seem to answer "Yes." Holding tightly to each others' hands, we begin walking...

Throughout the dream we alternate between communicating telepathically and actually talking. The sense of his presence and companionship never diminishes, but when he is quiet for a time I ask, "Are we really together or is it just my imagination?" He responds, "It doesn't work that way." I say, "Of course not. It's both!" We laugh about this, and keep walking... I feel we're heading somewhere and ask, "Where are we going?" He says he wants to go to (?) All I recall is that where we're headed begins with the letter "V". I wake.

Igor. I fell asleep really fast, and the next thing I remember is talking to Maria like it's normal, like we meet every day. I'm thinking it's supposed to be hard, but then I look at her and think it's normal... I wake with a strong feeling I need to go back to sleep... someone is calling me back. I close my eyes and I'm there. I start talking to Maria again, although most of the time we seem to communicate telepathically... I ask her if telepathy is a more advanced and more appropriate form of communication in dreams. She agrees it is, but the moment we try to do it on purpose we fail. We look at each other and wonder what we're thinking about... A few times I tell her, "What if this is a dream?" Even though we both know this is a dream, I still ask her that. I want to see her reaction and how it will confuse us. We laugh about it and keep walking... I feel we're going to a Viewpoint to see something nice.

The Man who kissed me in my dream was clad in the royal blue robes of a King. It is a source of great joy to me to obey the loving command of my Lord by reverently trying to "get used to" the blessings it pleases Him to bestow upon me. Filled with a humbling gratitude indistinguishable from a profound sense of well being, not a day goes by that I don't think about, and repeat to myself, what the Angel said to Mary, "For nothing is impossible with God"[24] and Christ's own words, "You will see greater things than this."[25]

Divine Speech

Dream of March 16, 2013

I'm in a clothing store, one of countless shops in an immense, sprawling mall. I've been here before, and I'm surprised I forgot about it, but maybe it only reminds me of another shop I've frequented. A woman walks up to me holding a sleeveless purple shirt on a hanger. "Look at this one!" she says excitedly, and my attention is immediately arrested, because it's one of those rare shirts that falls to mid thigh, which means I can wear my black yoga pants with it. I don't know the woman, but my surprise that she's helping me shop is superseded by my desire for more shirts like this one.

I say, "Listen closely. I'm asking you to get in touch with me whenever you see anymore shirts like this one, shirts that fall to just below here" I indicate the level on my thigh with one hand.

The woman assures me she will, and leading me over to the rack where she found the shirt, observes in disappointment, "Oh, it's the last one." I move along the rack, not seeing much of interest, but she rifles through some shirt-dresses hanging on the far right, and urges me to take a look. I do so, and suddenly she's gone, completely vanished from the store.

I head for the exit, thinking it very curious that my shopping guide simply disappeared, which is physically impossible. As I exit the store, and continue walking along the dimly lit passages of this underground mall, I become aware of the possibility that I can walk myself into lucidity. Then I spot my shopping guide a few yards away; her bright-green, long-sleeved sweater is unmistakable. I wasn't aware of her clothes before, which I seem to remember as having been dark and nondescript. She's bending over, and appears to be holding a bar of soap? Then she vanishes again, and reappears even farther away from me, on the other side of an avenue running parallel to the open air balcony I'm walking in. I hurry after her.

She has her back to me, and as I approach her, I become fully lucid at the same moment I ask her, "Who are you?"

Turning to face me, she begins speaking quickly, in a matter of fact tone of voice. I only remember two fragments of what she said: "A rush of cells to wash the scalpel... just looks down at this lump of dead matter." I understand she is telling me that as a character in my dream, she is merely a symbolic manifestation of physiological processes going on in my body while I sleep. This is *really* disappointing, even disturbing, and as she goes on relentlessly, I interrupt her to demand, "Are you fucking with me?"

My outburst silences her, and she gives me a little smile. "Yes," she admits, and now I see her clearly. Her bright green sweater has transformed into a shining, long-sleeved dark-green shirt with gold buttons, and her hair is not merely blonde, it is golden. She is young and attractive, in a distinguished, intelligent-looking way, and her expression is intriguingly animated. We begin walking side-by-side, heading for the exit as she communicates with me, but this part happens in a kind of dim, muted blur of colors.

The dream becomes vivid again when we step out into the night, and continue walking beneath a white, gently curving arbor that feels like it could go one forever. It is surrounded by a vast white circular building with tall arched doors and windows, all of them black now, lining its multiple stories. There are open spaces between the arbor and the building, in which I glimpse fountains and other artistic structures. I recognize this place, I've been here before in another lucid dream, in a different section, when the sun was shining. But tonight I have eyes only for my lovely Guide, whose golden hair frames her face in dense ringlets.

Keeping a firm grip on my right hand, she never stops speaking with fervent eloquence. I listen to her in wonder, for she is expressing herself in perfect, beautiful verse. I have never heard anyone actually speak like this; the closest approximation is an actor reciting Shakespeare. She uses no archaic words, she talks quickly and normally, and yet everything she says effortlessly emerges as exquisite prose-poetry, her conversation a verbal form of music. Fully wrapped up in the gravity of her intense gold and green presence, and acutely aware of the grip she has on my right hand, I dare to ask her, "Do all Angels talk like you?" Falling silent, she looks directly at me, and I slowly wake.

Later that night, I have another brief lucid dream. I'm sitting in a classroom, aware of being dressed in black, and facing a large window-screen of blue sky and clouds. Far below, on the surface of the earth, a black grid-map is displayed. The professor is mostly a black-clad presence to my right, where he stands just to one side of the window-screen. He is educating us on some of the unfortunate differences between how things are experienced where we are now vs. how they are experienced on earth, and how they must be "synched up." Just before waking, a genderless Voice says, "Hail Mary."

That morning I wrote: When I woke, I felt this lovely, divinely eloquent Angel had been sent to test me, and that, because I passed, I graduated to another level, literally expressed by the classroom I found myself in looking down at the earth. First, this Angel entered my non-lucid dream, and by her actions prompted me to slowly "wake up" to the fact that I was dreaming. She then began telling me, with an air of authority, that my dream, and by extension everything in it, was merely the result of physiological processes, a chemically induced hallucination cleverly fabricated by my brain. The two sentences I remembered from her speech after I woke were the most salient:

"A rush of cells to wash the scalpel... just looks down at this lump of dead matter..."

So descriptively vivid, and terrifying. Because of her lucid air of authority, for an awful moment in the dream I was forced to consider the possibility that materialistic science and atheists are right, and consciousness is a byproduct of the brain, nothing more. I experienced a moment of despair sharper than the scalpel she mentioned as I listened to what she seemed to be telling me, until my soul reacted with incredulous outrage. Her response to my challenge, and subsequent events, seem to indicate that she had, indeed, been testing me.

I perceived her as an Angel, but the Voice at the end of the dream clearly said, "Hail Mary."

Telepathic and Precognitive Dreams

The man in the classroom was educating us on some of the unfortunate differences between how things are experienced where we were, compared to how they are experienced on earth, and discussing how these two perspectives must be "synched up." I can only guess, but I have a strong feeling that lucid dreaming is already playing a vital role in this "synching up" process. Like many dreamers, lucid and non-lucid alike, I have experienced so-called telepathic, precognitive, and mutual or shared dreams in which information was received and/or exchanged that was later verified. I'm referring to information I was not privy to, and had not yet acquired, or even had the means of acquiring in waking reality. When I lucid dream, I'm aware of my soul transcending my body-brain even while remaining connected to it.

By the time I had this dream, I had already experienced numerous psi dreams involving loved ones as well as strangers. I had discovered that I can respond to a "call for help" in the dream space almost without knowing what I'm doing, and sometimes, it seems, without the person I'm helping consciously asking for help. Dream sharing is, for me, primarily about connecting with other souls, because we all benefit from it in ways we can scarcely imagine yet.

From my Lucid Dream Journal, October 18, 2013:

I'm walking down a crowded city street in broad daylight when I see a man in black robes running straight toward me, his arms stretched urgently out before him. "Help me! Help me!" he begs. "You can heal me! You can heal me! You're my healer!" I already know I'm dreaming and, hurrying over to him, I slip a supportive arm around his shoulders. I become rooted in the dream scene as I help him walk quickly in the direction he had been running. Trying to understand what happened to him, I lead him to temporary refuge against a wall where he crouches, weak and helpless.

I leave him there and go in search of something, perhaps his possessions. I seem to be walking on rocky, sandy cliffs. I remain conscious of being in a dream, and yet I also behave as though I've woken up as I begin telling some invisible presence about this lucid dream, broadcasting what I'm seeing as though communicating via a hidden microphone. I tell my contact how real everything looks, that it's like watching a huge screen TV, but not really because everything is in 3D and absolutely true to life. I watch troops climb and assemble on the upper level of a structure protecting a large compound. They are all lining up there in preparation for something, overlooking what might be the white tarmac of a large airbase or simply desert. I inform my invisible audience, "It's so realistic! I can't see their faces because the sun is behind them."

The troops are in full uniform, and suddenly I know it's wrong to call them troops because they don't look like American military; their uniforms are slightly different, they feel foreign to me, and there is a distinct circular dark-green patch on their sleeves. Many of the men are holding rifles, and they are all wearing caps of some kind.

After waking from this dream, I knew right away from the determinative of how it felt that it was "non-fiction". I searched key words online, and immediately found a breaking news story about Afghan insurgents who, at around the time I was dreaming, attacked a residential compound in which many important foreign officials and their families live. The International Security Assistance Force was called in, and their uniforms, logo patches and caps exactly matched those of the troops I saw in my dream.

I feel the man in the black robe may have been one of the two fatalities cited in the news report. Perhaps when people find themselves in extreme distress, and they send out a call for help, it is heard by one or more spiritually attuned dreamers.

Not long ago, I had a dream involving my deceased father (*with whom I have had several highly memorable lucid dreams*), my sister, and the person who, at the time, was her partner. My father and I were talking, seriously worried about my sister as we watched her drive away with her lover. Somehow, I knew their journey would take them from Route 81 to Carl Road.

Later that night, I had another dream in which I followed a trail of water to my study. I realized it had been left by my sister when her furious ghost, white with shock, confronted me in the kitchen yelling, "I'm dead! I can't believe I'm dead! I was drowned! I drowned! I can't believe it!" She also told me it had happened off Route 81 in Tiverton.

The next day, I phoned my sister (*she lives in another State, in an area I'm not at all familiar with*) and asked her if she ever made any sales calls off Route 81 in a place called Tiverton. She told me there is a Route 81 twenty minutes from her office, but that she had never heard of Tiverton. I asked her to be careful should she ever have to go there, and to be especially wary of

Carl Road. I didn't tell her I had seen her ghost, only that I had had a bad dream with her involving this location.

Two days later, I received a text message from my sister informing me that her current lover had grown up in a house off Route 81 in Tiverton, on Carl Road. This person's childhood had been extremely harsh and was, it began to seem, at the root of some of their destructive behavior patterns, in which my sister's own personality and happiness were "drowning". I'll never forget receiving that text message—an address from a dream displayed right there on my cell phone as actual physical fact. I knew next to nothing about my sister's new partner, and certainly nothing about their childhood home and experiences.

A specific address, relevant to the well-being of someone I love, was communicated to me in two dreams. All I did was choose to remember my dreams and respect them. I believe this is the most important choice any of us can make when it comes to our dreams. The effect my dream had on my sister and her former partner cannot be measured, but an intimate relationship that might have lingered unhealthily took a different direction, and they managed to preserve their friendship, until even that became too painful for my sister and they parted company.

Following Him

Dream of May 15, 2013

I see a Man, tall, attractive, wearing a black coat, somewhat pale face, hair a medium color. I follow Him, instantly and helplessly drawn to Him. When He sits down in a large space—a cross between an auditorium, a restaurant and a church—I sit down just behind Him and to his right, which gives me a clear view of His profile. I know He must be aware of me, but He says nothing. I become semi-lucid then as, looking around me, I suffer the self-conscious realization that I'm following a stranger around like an infatuated puppy, or a lost kitten.

I say, "Excuse me... I apologize for attaching myself to you like this... I've never done anything like this before... I hope you don't mind."

At once, He turns toward me, as if He has been aware of me all this time, and is happy to interact with me. He assures me that he doesn't mind at all, and as we smile at each other, I experience the exceptionally wonderful sense of being truly seen by Him, not just my physical appearance but all my uniquely beautiful depths. I know He can see my soul, and that He is pleased by what He sees.

He is eating something, so I shyly pull a treat out of my dog's bag, noticing then that my beloved pet is curled up asleep on the wooden bench to my left. Too late remembering that it's meant for dogs, I bite into the treat, painfully conscious of behaving like a shy teenager in front of a boy she has a huge crush on, but I can't help myself.

Observing me with a smile, He says I need to make a decision about what I'm going to do. Instantly, I set the dog treat down on the bench, and give Him my full attention. He tells me He wants to hear how I think our conversation would play out, with me imagining and speaking both our lines. I am completely daunted by the request, which is actually more of a command. How can I possibly imagine what He would say? He's here with me now, so why can't we just talk? Then He asks me if I don't think it's important, since I don't seem to want to really communicate with him, and immediately I reply, "Of course it's important. Words are the ambassadors of my soul!"

Looking immensely pleased by my statement, He turns to face in the opposite direction, and begins singing. Suddenly, a group of little children appear, accompanied by a woman I assume is their mother, and they all sit down across from Him. I watch their enraptured faces as the Man continues to sing in a quiet, yet effortlessly powerful, voice...

That morning I wrote: The fact that I bit into a dog treat relates to how I think about my ego-self being like a dog in relation to my Guardian Lords, who love and protect, care for, train and discipline my soul, without me understanding how it all works, just as my dog doesn't comprehend the more subtle dimensions of *my* life. Maybe this Guardian Lord is suggesting I am capable of comprehending more than I think I can, hence His request that I recite both sides of our possible conversation. The key is in the statement I made which prompted Him to begin singing: "Words are the ambassadors of my soul." It reminds me of a lucid dream I had not long ago in which a dream character said, "Her soul is a song on the wind."

In hindsight, I feel both extremely foolish and ashamed. After more than two years, I still didn't understand who *He* was. I was too enthralled by the adventure of lucid dreaming to notice what is so obvious to me now. It's no wonder that in this dream, where I followed Him around like a lost puppy, my Lord chided me for not really wanting to communicate with Him.

> Jesus did not lift up His voice nor make Himself heard in the street. He did not cry aloud, but was calm and quiet. People came to Him for the Truth. But the things of the flesh are so insistent, so clamorous. Before you are up in the morning, they are clamoring at you, trying to get you interested in buying what they are selling or doing what they have decided you should do. Everybody is singing to you, urging you, pushing you— by example, by precept, by instruction, by advertising and urging—trying to get you to go certain ways and do certain things.
>
> Our Lord is never intrusive, but the things of the world are intrusive. Here is the point I am trying to make: If you are going to give attention to the things of God and save your own soul, you are going to have to have a good intention, a good resolution, and then see to it that you do it...
>
> God meant it when He gave us the Law. Christ meant it

when He died and rose on the third day. The Holy Ghost means it when He quietly speaks to your heart.[26]

Chapter Six – Engaged

I love the way the Lord
whispers endearments to me
through angels of synchronicity
when I'm both awake and asleep
all I need do is look and listen
to be so blessed every day

I became conscious of the sun's warmth
pressed up behind me as I composed
this prayer-poem while walking my dog
and felt the Spirit's arm around my shoulders
The Presence of Love my constant inspiration

The Book of Life

Dreams of June 13, 2013

Between 2:10 and 2:45, I had one of those rare, exceptionally real-feeling, semi-lucid dreams. It's the middle of the night, but I'm up in the Den with my Shih Tzu, Arthur. It feels very real; I'm certain I'm awake. I ask Arthur, "You want to go for a quick pee before we go back to bed?" He looks delighted; this is a special treat, because he always sleeps straight through the night. We run happily together into the Sun Room, where I stop abruptly and pick him up, crouching down as I look out the windows in surprise. A small military plane has just landed in our driveway, and unloaded young troops I distinctly see crossing the yard just outside. They appear to be practicing night maneuvers, and convey no sense of danger or urgency, only a perfectly disciplined purpose.

My eyes are drawn to the face of a young woman in the line. Her expression sober, she is holding a rifle as she stares straight ahead of her into the darkness, obviously not afraid of it. I admire how she is up in the dead of the night—a time I associate with feeling weak and vulnerable, when life's fears gang up on my mortal self—even as I identify with her calm, focused, wide awake control, qualities I have embraced through my lucid dreaming practice.

Arthur is squirming in my arms, impatient to go out as I promised him he could, but I can't let him because large dogs have accompanied the squadron, canine soldiers. A few feet beyond the door, in the middle of our courtyard-driveway, a large black dog is standing next to the tall, broad-shouldered silhouette of a troop commander.

Somehow, it makes sense that a piece of the army has chosen our property for a training mission. I'm actually pleased, even honored, to be able to assist our troops in this way. I'm crouching inside the room as I look out the windows, keeping respectfully out of sight. Abruptly, Stinger is kneeling beside me...

The next thing I know, we're standing before the androgynous commander, who is seated at a small desk speaking to us, and holding a book bound in fine red leather that is central to what he/she is telling us about in a serious, but very animated way. I sit down with the large book, and become semi-lucid as I wonder at how real all this seems; a part of me understands I'm dreaming. The book feels perfectly solid as I run my fingertips along the smooth red leather cover, and then, opening it, over slightly raised sketches drawn in black with red highlights. I remain conscious of the invisible troops surrounding the Sun Room watching me, and wonder if they think I'm feigning my rapt interest in the book, but I'm definitely not. Although in waking reality I would feel self conscious about being the center of attention, in the dream I'm perfectly relaxed, and genuinely engrossed in the book.

The commander tells Stinger he/she is leaving the book with us, so that we can make an exact replica, not merely a copy. I'm surprised, and understand this is an honor, an expression of complete trust in our stewardship of this highly important object. I know, without being told, that what I'm holding in my hands, with such visual and tactile presence, is the metaphysical tale of my soul and its relationship with God, which entails confronting the devil, even though the only figure illustrated is hers/mine. God is invisibly present all around her on the white pages, while the devil takes form only in small details that manifest on her body, such as mouse-like ears, or little horns growing from her head. She is drawn in a flowing yet precise fashion, her face and profile masterfully rendered and animated.

Approximately halfway, or a little more, into the book, it seems to end, and in a sense it does, for the time being, because there are only white pages beyond that point. But as I continue flipping through the book, I realize the pages are all illustrated, or will be. The final page shows her/me standing and smiling into the book, the look on her face absolutely joyful.

Later in the night, deep in another dream, I have a false awakening. Wearing only a long white shift, I get out of bed, and crawl on my hands and knees through a garden pavilion to the feet of a man I know is a King, and also my husband. He too is clad all in white, and I am eager to tell him about my dream, but He orders me back to bed, wordlessly letting me know there is still enough time in the night for me to continue dreaming...

I enter a bedroom I know belongs to me. The door is large and dense, made of a dark, intricately carved wood with a foreign look and feel to it. I desire to close the door all the way to shut out the sounds of the crowd milling outside, but I also need to leave it slightly ajar so as not to lock someone out—Mami, who quickly enters the room and sits down at the table. She watches me, a smile on her face, as I quickly begin writing my lucid dream on a dark, greenish-brown cloth with a pencil-stick that is nearly the same color. I begin very near the top edge of the cloth, which is spread out on the table, but it begins fraying, the pressure of my penmanship loosening the threads to reveal their varied colors as they curl up, rising like plant seedlings that give the cloth an even more earthy appearance. Concerned about losing my dream notes, I carefully rip the layer of cloth off the more solid wood beneath, and continue writing.

I become aware of a handsome blonde man standing to my right when he smiles, and turns on a television hanging on the wall. It seems the show he and Mami have been waiting for is just beginning. I grasp the contents of the broadcast in the form of a vision—my new dress, standing upright on the edge of a bright white stage, made specifically for me, and the most beautiful garment I have ever seen. The cloth looks soft and supple even though it is completely covered by shining, geometrically cut precious stones of every color, with gold, blue and red hues predominate. The garment begins high at the neck and falls, gently formfitting, all the way to the floor. It gleams as though alive, but is the exact opposite of a cold reptilian skin. I can scarcely believe this dress is meant for me.

Just before waking, I see the tree-bordered gravel country road I walk on almost every day. An ageless dark-haired woman dressed in flowing white, is standing on the right side of the road. Clearly visible against the dark-green foliage, she is looking directly at me.

That morning I wrote: Making an exact replica of the Book of Life could symbolize how every soul experiences the same journey of spiritual growth in its own unique way. These dreams were so rich that I don't want to dissect them, but here goes: The soul is akin to a Troop Commander, the squadron of thoughts and feelings under its direction—the soldier of our mortal personality fighting for the ultimate freedom of spiritual enlightenment.

The female soldier, walking fearlessly through the darkness outside my house, makes me think of how I often deliberately wake up and walk around in the dead of night as part of my lucid dreaming practice, known as Wake Back To Bed. As a lucid dreamer, I do not fear the darkness of sleep, or all the dangerous thoughts and feelings hiding in my so-called subconscious. All the battles I fight are with myself, for a greater purpose.

Carl Jung is the author of the famous *Red Book*, which my husband gave me as a belated Christmas present shortly after we moved into our dream home. In Jungian analysis, marriage symbolizes the potential for union between God and the individual.

◐

I will admit that I felt encouraged, and rather proud of myself after this dream, singled out by "higher powers" for some sort of spiritual promotion. This dream seemed to indicate that, at long last, I was making some real progress in my life-long battle with the demons of doubts and fears, and all the character weaknesses they breed, which can become our soul's worst enemies. I don't think I was wrong about that, but I do see now that the Book I was given to keep, and make my own, is *the* Book, the Holy Bible, the Word of God. In my dream, I felt God's Presence on every pure white page, but perhaps one reason so many pages were blank is because I had not yet begun reading it for myself.

> "The reason Christ comes to meet us in Scripture is not merely to inform us, but to transform us. Therefore, the

spiritual understanding of Scripture, or the allegorical meaning, is never just something detached, historical or catechetical. God speaks to us through Scripture and awaits personal response. Spiritual understanding of Scripture and the process of conversion are one and the same... We don't reach out to take the meaning of the text and try to apply it to our lives. Rather, when we put ourselves before God in the Bible, the Spirit that dwells in the words reaches out and assimilates us to Himself. God's word is alive and efficacious... This power... is a testimony of their divine origin."[27]

I can now sum up my dream in a few words: Read the Word of God, and feel it come alive in your heart as it speaks directly and personally to your soul.

In my dream, the Book was also meant for my husband, and by extension for everyone, but I proudly claimed it all for myself. The Holy Spirit has been extremely patient with me, for the truth is that, in certain respects, I have always been vain, and considered myself extra special, God only knows why. Each of us has a personal relationship with God and his Word, so what I held in my hands in the dream was, indeed, the journey of my soul. But I conveniently made light of the several illustrations where the devil's continued influence on me was expressed by little red horns on my head, and other telling details. Nevertheless, the end result was positive—I stood looking back into the Book smiling beatifically.

It took much longer than it should have, but I am at last properly educating myself with God's own Words. When I read the Gospels, I feel the Lord speaking directly to my soul, and it often makes me cry for joy, mingled with shame and regret, at how long I denied myself His intimate Presence and support.

> "Like many, I thought I could bootstrap my way to an understanding of spiritual truths through my reasoning powers alone, largely unaware of the actual content of God's special revelation in the Bible... I was constantly seeking the truth, but usually through my own feeble efforts and presumptuous ponderings, and without studying the Bible itself or examining Christian doctrine more carefully... When it finally dawned on me that I was holding in my hands a written communication from the God of the universe, my life changed."[28]

I see the spectacular jeweled dress as representing my Spirit, which is one with God, the source, the eternal "fabric" of all manifest experience. For me, the dress expresses the marriage of heaven and earth, spirituality with sensuality, the Creator with His creation.

> "The cutting and shaping of precious stones signifies the soul shaped from the rough, irregular, dark stone into the gem, regular in shape and reflecting divine light... Jewels symbolize hidden treasures of knowledge and truth, but also earthly love and riches"[29]

When I was writing down my dream about the Book during my false awakening, my pencil cut into the fabric like a seamstress working on a living dress. Almost exactly one year after this dream, I came upon the following passage in the autobiography of Saint Therese of Lisieux:

> "O my God! I don't ask you to make Profession. *I will wait as long as you desire,* but what I don't want is to be the cause of my separation from You through my fault. I will take great care, therefore, to make a beautiful dress enriched with priceless stones, and when You find it sufficiently adorned, I am certain all the creatures in the world will not prevent You from coming down to me to unite me to Yourself forever, O my Beloved!"[30]

Re-Confirmation

Dreams of July 4, 2013

I'm lying on my left side in the dark when I feel that inner shift, followed by a sensation almost like someone spooning me from behind, and I understand what's happening—I'm primed to have on Out of Body Experience.[31] I quickly sit up, yet I can't quite disconnect from my physical form lying on the bed. I suffer a false awakening then, disappointed that I failed to leave my body after coming so close. I part the curtains over the glass doors, and am surprised to see that it's already morning. Wow, I must have slept like a log. I also notice the door isn't locked, and carefully turn the handle until I feel it click into place. I get up, and go about my morning business, feeling a little confused at how deeply I slept without interruption....

I find myself standing in the Den, instantly aware that I'm out of body in the middle of the night. I'm sweeping clean an old doormat using an old broom. Just outside the glass doors, behind the green curtains, I sense a crowd of very nasty people who, also sensing my presence, are attempting to break in. I don't feel terribly threatened by them; I'm confident my door is locked, my space secure. These beings are more annoying than frightening, but I still don't want them inside, or even so close to me, so I command impatiently, "Be gone, demons!"

In high pitched voices, they echo me mockingly, "Be gone demons! Be gone demons!"

I repeat the command, "Be gone, demons!"

Again they mock me, "Be gone demons! Be gone demons!"

Changing my tactic, I say, "Poof!" intending a brilliant flash of light to manifest outside and drive them away. Between the cracks in the curtains, I see this doesn't work, but I try again, and again, until the darkness outside is suffused for an instant by a bright golden light, after which the demonic crowd at the door is no longer there.

A seamless transition to sitting lucidly outside at night at a wooden bar adjoining the Den. I'm facing a slender, and still attractive, older woman. She is very elegant, her silver-white hair falling to her shoulders where it thickens in a smooth old-fashioned wave. I know her very well, and as we talk companionably, the subject of the Christening jewelry my mother gave me comes up. *(In waking reality, I received no such jewelry.)* I produce—or rather, I am mysteriously handed from the darkness to my left—a pair of little heart-shaped earrings made of a smooth yellow material, ivory or jade, with miniature dark crosses set in their centers. The earrings are part of a set, and I give them to the woman.

I am then handed, again from the darkness to my left, a matching necklace made of the same smooth natural material, which I also give to the woman. She is familiar with the lovely jewelry, and seems to want it, seems to *need* me to give it to her.

There is a third and final Christening item I am handed by the darkness—a shirt. I pass it over to my companion, and she promptly, surprising me, slips it on. The garment is transparent except for a pearl-white border along the collar bone, from which it falls straight and fine over the flesh-colored shirt she is wearing beneath it. The garment fits her perfectly, and makes her look, despite her age, exceptionally elegant and lovely. She sits up straighter, smiling at me with happy pleasure and, I feel, renewed vigor. The ethereal Christening shirt makes her as beautiful as she can be, and I sense a Man who loves her, and who she will be able to "go out" with now. I declare, "You look beautiful. Keep it, please, it looks ridiculous on me." I imagine the shirt is too small for me, almost like a doll's shirt I can't possibly fit into anymore. Her smile deepening, she replies, "I do believe I will."

Some time after this exchange, I'm back in the Den, sweeping again, but now the doors are open to a gray morning light. I'm directing quantities of dirt out of the room, piling it into evidence, which includes strands of my hair, and the flesh-colored shirt the older woman was wearing beneath the new transparent one I gave her. I'm not sure what this is evidence of, but I'm compelled to present it to some supreme authority, which I'm expecting to arrive at any moment.

The Man who in the dream I felt loved the woman—with Who she was free to be with now and realize her full beauty—is, of course, Christ our Lord. This is obvious to me now, but when I woke up that morning, I seemed to recognize the woman as Susie S. Mayo, the one whose epitaph I was led to by a dream: LOVE LIGHT MY WAY TO GOD. I thought I had perhaps interacted with her soul again. In the dream, I saw myself as being bigger than her physically, and also more fully developed mentally and emotionally, which is why I passed the Christening gifts to her, as though they were mere toys I no longer needed because my soul had outgrown them. It wasn't until recently, when reading this dream again, that its sacred significance fell sharply and fully into place in my mind and heart.

The woman from my dream looked very much as I do now. About three years ago, I stopped dyeing my hair black and began letting it grow out silver-white. Recently, I cut it short, to just shoulder-length, where it curves naturally. I was handed

Christening gifts from the darkness—from the night, during which we sleep and dream—and though I thought I was returning them to a more naive, less sophisticated woman, like toys I had outgrown, I was actually returning them to myself and my soul. I didn't realize this at the time, so in the dream I seemed to be sitting across from someone else. My conscious mind still thought of Christianity as too limiting, but my soul already knew the truth.

The Holy Spirit was with me that night; it was not my own powers that banished the demons at my door, even though I let myself think so. Yet it was precisely the arrogant delusion of self-sufficiency I was sweeping out of my soul once and for all.

Heavenly Games

Dream of July 14, 2013

I get up off my lucid dreaming bed in the Den. My family is also up, for I hear my parents in the living room. Then suddenly my brother (still a little boy in the dream) runs into the room and stands beside my bed. I look at him and exclaim, "Wait, you're up too early, you would never get up so early. This is still a dream!" I walk happily into the pitch-black living room, where Papi's silhouette is standing. At that moment, Mami's silhouette walks out of the kitchen.

I announce, "Estamos soñando. Este es un Sueño." ("We're dreaming. This is a dream.")

Mami tells Papi, "Es verdad." (It's true.)

I say, "Vamos a caminar afuera." ("Let's go walk outside") and together the three of us step out the front door.

Far away the black sky is filled with brilliant white stars, multitudes of them, so incredibly beautiful and heartwarming. It doesn't matter that the porch, and the world, are still impenetrably dark. Looking over my right shoulder, to where my parents are standing just behind me, I deliberately relish the Spanish language of my childhood as I announce, "Voy a volar con mi mamá y mi papá. Vamos!" ("I'm going to fly with my mother and father. Let's go!") I take Mami's left hand with my right hand, and we promptly rise effortlessly up into the sky, with Papi following just behind us. I look at Mami and declare, "Qué bella!" ("How beautiful!") for she looks to be in her late twenties again. Yet her face, so beloved and familiar, also seems a little different, a little like another woman's, like the face of a Saint.

At one point, Papi, who is just above me, becomes horizontal as he falls down toward me, but I laughingly support his weight, and help him straighten himself up again. We pass bare black tree branches and, as we slowly gain altitude, I see that at least two trees are occupied by a single person poised in the topmost branches, their posture evocative of Native American scouts scanning the land below. They are wearing what appear to be light-brown deer-skin outfits, and are facing in the direction in which my family and I are flying.

The sounds of life are an ambient music in the night emanating from everywhere, endlessly rich and yet also deeply subtle. I even hear what sounds like one of our old laying hens clucking excitedly somewhere below me. I extend my hand toward her in delight before thinking—Oh that's ridiculous, I'm not going to cuddle up with my old chicken right now!

Looking up again, I'm presented with the astonishing sight of a city like no earthly city. Two immense white buildings rise across from each other, but they are rendered almost in two dimensions, their windows, and the people leaning out of them, much larger than they can realistically be. Everywhere I look, the perspective changes and shifts, so that some people look colossal while others appear smaller. The edifices are white, but the people—their skin, hair and clothes—are all vividly colorful.

High above this surrealistic city scene, I suddenly make out what appear to be spaceships! Alien life forms visiting earth?! The spaceships resemble vessels from the new version of the sci-fi series *Battlestar Galactica,* and seem to be firing at each other. But my dismay lasts only an instant when I realize that what is actually issuing from the ships are spheres of bright red, gold and silver lights which look, for all the world, like glittering Christmas ornaments made of fireworks growing in size as they descend toward earth and transform into... toys! Toys are raining down from heaven! I notice then that the theme of "play" is featured everywhere as I spot a much larger-than-life little girl holding a baseball bat where she leans out of a great window.

Gazing around me in amazement, I wonder how this can possibly be the future, even though it is obviously not the present, because there is no sign of any of the evils currently plaguing our world. Everything appears to be perfectly all right as toys keep raining down from the heavens! Some of the toys are so big—a white submarine-like spaceship, for example—I'm almost afraid of being crushed by them, but they are falling toward earth as lightly as snowflakes in a magical storm. I have *never* experienced anything like this in a lucid dream! Scarcely believing my eyes, I wake.

I did not write anything about this dream after I woke up, feeling words would only detract from the sense of profound hope it filled me with. It's message is even clearer to me now—our Father loves us, and if we in turn love Him with all our heart, and truly live our lives as God's children, His gifts to Us are worlds without end through the Divine play of Creation.

"You must love the Lord your God with all your heart, all your soul, all your strength, and all your mind." And "Love your neighbor as yourself." Luke 10:27[32]

An Invitation

Dream of July 18, 2013

Stinger and I are entering the expansive grounds of an outdoor event honoring people who have achieved excellence in their chosen art form, and where I will be reading something I wrote. As we walk beneath a curved stone archway, passing through deep shadow on our way to a sunlit hilltop, a handsome Young Man with blonde hair walks directly up to us, and invites us to his second floor balcony where he would like us to smoke some herb together. Then he steps back into the shadows, and I lose sight of him.

Out in the open air, it is a beautiful sunny day. Stinger and I make ourselves comfortable on the summit of the hill, and I look around me with interest. Far to my left, I glimpse a baseball game in progress, the young players currently the best of the best. Directly before me, but several yards away, smiling young female gymnasts in sleeveless white "swimsuits" are rehearsing an amazing floor show. I watch in awe as, one at a time, they glide straight through the air, from right to left, their bodies parallel to the ground in fish-like defiance of gravity.

I become aware that Stinger is no longer sitting slightly behind me, but has apparently gone off to smoke with the Young Man who invited us to join Him. I'm a bit surprised, and annoyed, that he simply left without telling me, especially since the invitation was extended to both of us. A moment later, I spot my husband, the blonde Man at his side, stepping out onto a small stone balcony jutting from the building that forms one side of this beautiful place. Rising, I head left, and begin walking parallel to the building. Remembering the directions the Young Man gave us, I'm confident I can find the door I seek, and there it is; I clearly recognize it.

I enter an expansive foyer comprised of various materials—stone, concrete, wood, and metal—with an initially confusing set of possible directions to take. But almost at once, I discern dark wooden steps leading up, and to the right, and I know this is the correct path to follow.

Ascending to a second floor corridor, I proceed deeper into the building, which feels rather like a very old university. A male student passes me, but otherwise I'm alone. The place is dimly lit and obviously centuries old. I experience a visceral sense of time, of a multitude of events and moments still residing in the stone and in the wood, moments that all have new life in the present. And yet at the same time, there is no real distinction between past and present and future; it is all one increasingly rich *now*.

At the end of the corridor, I turn right, confident the room I'm looking for is coming up on my left. I find it... Abruptly, I'm outside again, and walking up the steps of a small front porch. I move quietly, mischievously sneaking up on Stinger and the Young Man where they are sitting cross legged on the floor, their backs to me. Stepping between them, I smile down at our Host as he looks up at me. Suddenly, my little dog, Arthur, is in my arms, urgently sitting up in my grasp as, staring fervently at the Young Man, he makes a supreme effort to speak. His jaw working passionately, he emits high-pitched, intensely compressed words which only partially emerge, and *almost* make sense. I wonder hopefully if our Host will be impressed by my dog, even as I realize Arthur is behaving this way because our Host is *very* special. All I know for certain is that I want to stay here with Him; there is no other place I would rather be.

I settle in, and at some point "wake" with a start to the

awareness of holding a sheaf of papers in my hands, a long piece of writing I don't remember having begun, but which I clearly did. The paper are marked in red ink with my first initial edits, which I haven't keyed in yet. I'm pleased to be working on what appears to be another book, but for now I set it aside in order to enjoy the profoundly peaceful pleasure of being where I am.

Intent on retrieving something from the grass nearby, Stinger momentarily leaves the porch—the threshold of the Young Man's living space—while I happily focus on our host as He bends over what looks like a potted pea plant. He is wrapping one of the long fine shoots, sent out by the plant in search of purchase, tightly around one of His fingers. Holding it there for a long moment, he explains to me what He's doing, "Training it to grow in the right direction."

Utterly content simply to continue watching Him, I notice a man with long hair climbing onto the adjoining balcony. I'm startled to recognize my own husband, a fellow member of this community of free spirits who care not at all what the world thinks of them. Then I spot another man approaching from the direction I arrived. I smile politely at him as he walks part way up the steps, and then stops to stare up at me in what strikes me as a very unfriendly way.

I turn away from the dangerous looking stranger, and as our wonderful Host bends over another task, I focus lucidly on his long-sleeved, forest-green button-down shirt, gently tucked into slate-green pants. Seeing him as clearly as I perceive in waking reality, I notice the slightly worn texture of his clothing, which suggests He bought his shirt at a thrift store, and that He doesn't have much money, but simply by looking at him I know he doesn't need, or want, more money. His clothing is slightly threadbare, yet of the finest quality, and He would look beautiful in anything. I can almost *smell* this Man He is so absolutely present, and all I want is to remain here with Him. When He stands up straight, looking past me with a small, grim smile on his lips, I watch, enthralled, as He raises His right hand, and throws a small, sharp blade at the evil looking man hovering on the steps. The stranger succeeds in dodging it, but seems unable to come any closer.

I remain standing beside our Host, and there is no doubt in my heart He is my new dream partner. *This* is the Man I am destined to dream with in the future, and forever...

My alarm goes off. I wake with a start, feeling disoriented, and utterly bereft. Only a moment ago, I was vividly somewhere else with someone so wonderful, so special, it fills me with despair to think I have no way of contacting him in waking reality.

That morning I wrote: I have the very strong feeling that a specific living person I am meant to do dream work with was foretold, for lack of a less dramatic word, in this dream. I also feel a new book gestating inside me, one I will soon begin writing, the one I was reading on the porch in my dream.

I didn't realize it then, but I had already begun writing this book simply by keeping a journal of all of my lucid and semi-lucid dreams.

I couldn't bear the thought of never seeing this Young Man again, of never even meeting Him. I was already in love with Him, and He didn't even exist?! It was inconceivable! So strong was my desire to find Him, so intensely bereft did I feel when he vanished from my life as I woke up, that I asked my husband to purchase the url "lucidfriendfinder.com". Many lucid dreamers feel that some of the people they encounter and interact with in their dreams may be individuals alive on earth today, and after this dream, I was on fire to help launch a future—which couldn't possibly happen fast enough for me—where lucid dreamers would be able to search for and, ideally, meet people they had encountered in the dream space. My husband is a Botanist, but also a computer informatics and data specialist, and for several evenings over drinks we discussed the various algorithms required for such a website, which would need to compare and analyze dozens of dreams to begin with, and potentially thousands, in intricate detail. A few months later, when I began working with my current dream partners, I added the Blog "Dreamshares" to the "lucidfriendfinder" url. Dreamshares[33] is where we post our shared dreaming experiences. Its parent site, Lucidfriendfinder.com, is under construction.

This dream prompted me to grow in the right direction, for I truly feel I am doing God's will through my ongoing exploration of lucid dream sharing. The Holy Spirit is everywhere, including in our dreams. The Bible is filled with special, life-changing and prophetic dreams.

> "In New Testament times, divine revelation is presumed to occur in visions and dreams, and such inner experience is treated as a normal way of God's revelation... According to Luke in the Book of Acts, dreams and visions occurred frequently and at important moments in the life of the early Christian community... Others among the early disciples, such as the deacon Stephen who was martyred, reported dreams and visions. Dreams and visionary material were treated seriously and given much authority in the nascent Church... Today, few in religious ministry are trained in dreamwork skills. On the other hand, we know from our workshop and counseling experiences that ministers, priests, sisters, and lay people all have vivid dreams, sometimes with clear religious symbolism."[34]

Dreams and symbolism are inseparable from our innate creativity as the children of God. We all have dreams, whether or not we remember them. Unfortunately, many of us have been encouraged since childhood to ignore our dreams; to dismiss them as random synaptic firings of our brains busily rehashing the day or performing other subconscious maintenance.

The phrase "It's just a dream" has had a deleterious effect on our inclination to remember our dreams by implying that we don't need to respect or pay attention to them. However, had we been told as children that it's important we try to remember our dreams, and that becoming lucid in our dreams can help us conquer fears and positively impact our waking life, more people would probably remember their dreams, and become lucid in them more often. Fortunately, it's never too late to begin giving our dreams the attention and appreciation they deserve.

> "Though reflected outward in billions of manifest forms and activities and individual awarenesses, underneath, all are enlivened by the same light, the light of awareness. While apparently apart from others and apparently separate from objects, nature, and space, this awareness connects us at a deeper level. In lucid dreaming, we can consciously access this knowing and begin to demonstrate the existence of this profoundly connected realm."[35]

Reading my dream of the Young Man again now, it seems obvious to me who He was, regal and beautiful in His humble thrift store clothing, Who He *is* forever—Jesus Christ. My dog spoke in tongues, desperate to express his adoration of the Man in whose presence we were so blessed to find ourselves.

"Ascending to a second floor corridor, I proceed deeper into the building, which feels rather like a very old university... centuries old... I experience a visceral sense of time, of a multitude of events and moments still residing in the stone and in the wood, moments that all have new life in the present. And yet at the same time, there is no real distinction between past and present and future; it is all one

increasingly rich now... this community of free spirits who care not at all what the world thinks of them."

The undying spirit, the living Word, of Christianity.

> "We didn't have to be alive when Jesus was on this earth in order to profit from His message. Though He was here but a brief time, His words, in Scripture, endure forever."[36]

"When He stands up straight, looking past me with a small, grim smile on his lips, I watch, enthralled, as He raises His right hand, and throws a small, sharp blade at the evil looking man hovering on the steps. The stranger succeeds in dodging it, but seems unable to come any closer."

> "So humble yourselves under the mighty power of God, and at the right time he will lift you up in honor. Give all your worries and cares to God, for he cares about you. Stay alert, watch out for your great enemy, the devil. He prowls around like a roaring lion, looking for someone to devour." 1 Peter 5.6-8[37]

'Oh, the devil, the devil!' we say, when we might be saying 'God! God!' and making the devil tremble. Of course we might, for we know he cannot move a finger unless the Lord permits it... I am quite sure I am more afraid of people who are themselves terrified of the devil than I am of the devil himself. For he cannot harm me in the least.[38]

Chapter Seven – The Holy Spirit

My soul obeys the Holy Spirit
I am His lover
His spouse
His homemaker
and administrative assistant

I no longer think it's all up to me
I know everything hinges on my soul –
a unique relationship with God's Love
Host of all perceptions of feeling
my intuition the depth of His kisses
my circumstances His ardent caresses
desirable even when hard or painful
instructing me in what is true forever –
the Creative Spirit abiding within me

"Love, love, love, without love, where would I be!?"

These are the opening and closing lines of a poem I wrote on the cold stone floor of the entrance foyer of our house in Caracas, Venezuela, where my father was stationed with U.S.A.I.D. for sixteen months when I was nine-years-old. I'll never forget that moment; I think of it often. For me, life has always been about love.

When I was sixteen-years-old, after watching the mini-series *Jesus of Nazareth*, I walked to our church one afternoon. It was almost empty, and as I sat there, I wept, because I knew in my heart what I truly wanted to do with my future—I wanted to give my life to Christ and be His bride. It was the most wonderful, and the most terrifying, realization.

Eventually, I got up and walked home, where I told my grandmother that I wanted to be a nun. The blend of dismay and admiration on her face almost made me feel I had grown another head, with which I was about to devour all her long-cherished marital hopes for me. My Abuelita was a devout Catholic; every night she prayed to the Virgin Mary, whose picture she kept by her bed for as long as I can remember, and yet she didn't look at all happy that I suddenly felt this way.

Though I fervently answered her questions and addressed her objections as best I could, the following day I confessed to myself that I wanted to be a nun because I was in love with Christ the way a woman loves and desires a man. And, to a much lesser degree, I felt the same way about his apostles; the actors portraying them in the film were to me the sexiest of men. I thought—I can't be a nun, because I love Christ sensually as well as spiritually.

I wonder now if a handsome man virile with the Holy Spirit had come into my life early on, and I had become his wife, if I could have been as perfectly passionate with him as I was meant to be. But that was not the long, self-indulgent path I followed, increasingly under the thrall of sexual desires and temptations that would have made Saint Augustine blush.

Yet it was always love that drove me; I was always searching for that perfect Man and Master worthy of my absolute submission and complete devotion. God well knew this, and a year after I entered menopause, He opened for me the door of lucid dreaming, through which the Holy Spirit entered my soul.

> "God does not bestow these favors on certain souls because they are more holy than others who do not receive them, but to manifest His greatness, as in the case of Apostle Paul and Mary, and that we may glorify Him in His creatures... There is no danger here of shocking those for whom I am writing by treating such matters, for they know and believe that God gives even greater proofs of His love. I am certain that if any one of you doubts the truth of this, God will never allow her to learn it by experience, for He desires that no limits should be set to His work. Therefore, never discredit them because you yourselves are not led in the same manner."[39]

Inspiration

Dream of August 17, 2013

I'm in a public place I can best describe as an airport terminal, in one of the more intimate, partially enclosed waiting areas closest to the glass walls. I don't actually see planes, but I distinctly sense the presence of great wings, and the power to travel. There is a single row of chairs all attached to each other, and I am sitting in one of them. There are many people in this waiting area, some seated like myself, some coming and going, others milling around in a relaxed manner.

This part of my dreaming lasts for what feels like a very long time. I can't remember how I got here, but for a while now I have been blissfully aware of the presence of my beloved Guardian Lord. The first thing I vividly remember is Him slipping into the seat on my left, and presenting me with a sheaf of papers, something written by Him, but which I am being given the task of transcribing. There is another stabilizing male presence seated silently on my right, the mysterious Agent who has put me in the position to be granted this great honor.

As my Guardian Lord holds the papers in front of us (it is actually more like a non-physical projection) He places his right hand on the top of my left thigh as though casually, but his hand remains there. I can scarcely believe it, and I wait for the terrible disappointment I will experience when He moves His hand away, but His hand remains very deliberately where it is. He seems to be letting me know that I am not imagining He desires me as much as I desire Him. Then He draws my attention to the letters **F C**, which are distinctly written by hand above the typed text. He explains to me what they stand for, and I quickly assure Him I can easily remember it, that I am up to the task.

It feels like the middle of the night as He rises from the chair beside mine, but doesn't leave the area. I have eyes only for Him as He moves closer to the glass partition before me, where he meets with several people. He is wearing a dark-blue jacket over a white dress shirt and black slacks, and His presence is indistinguishable from my happiness, from the glow in my heart making me feel as though my soul is expanding with love and desire, and that there is nothing more important in the universe than this feeling.

I can scarcely believe it when He comes and sits down beside me again. Smiling down at me, He says something as I gaze up at him longingly. Then, without my noticing the gesture, He pulls a protective cowl over both our heads, so that our faces are very close, and kisses me. The kiss feels very real, and lasts for a long moment as our lips part gently against each others. Pulling back slightly, He smiles down at me reassuringly before blessing me with another lingering kiss. I don't remember what He says afterward, if anything, but His expression as He gazes directly into my eyes is more than sufficiently eloquent.

Finding my voice, I confess, "I've loved you since I first saw you! You reminded me of ancient Egypt, of someone very special I must have known!"

He replies with a question, "How did you know I would feel the same way?"

I get feeling He is teasing me, and not wanting him to think I'm some New Age flake, I clarify how I felt about Him in particular, "I knew the Truth finally had a champion!"

The sheltering cowl no longer over our heads, He rises, but remains in the vicinity as I stay where I am, watching Him, and cherishing the incredible fact that He kissed me twice! I have been semi-lucid all this time, but much too thrilled by what is happening to feel any desire to assume full conscious control of the dream.

My beloved Guardian Lord eventually moves to a space just

beyond the waiting area where I'm sitting, somewhere behind me to the right, but when I look over my shoulder, I can still see him through the glass wall. He is standing, surrounded by a group of His people, in a space between inside and outside. He smiles over at me, then issues a silent command, and I suffer the impression He is deliberately playing a little joke on me as handsome young men begin filing past me. Moving from left to right in my Lord's direction, each man brushes against my knees while making an elaborate show of almost dropping the item he is carrying on top of me. I remember a mirror, a piece of furniture, and a large chest, beautiful gilded treasures that seem taken from a palace. The heavy treasures hover above me for a threatening moment as I raise my arms to shield my head, cringing in my seat, aware that I'm not in any real danger, but playing the game. I witness the scene from my Lord's perspective as well as my own, "pulsing" from one point of view to another, as though we are one heart with two separate sets of eyes. The final treasure is a live cheetah, and I suffer a twinge of real concern when it pounces onto the chair beside mine, yet I know it won't hurt me, and that it's friendly behavior toward me is actually an honor.

As I phase out of the dream, I immediately think about how in ancient Egypt, at least during the New Kingdom, all the personal treasures the deceased chose to bring with him into the afterlife were carried into the tomb, one by one, by a procession of young men walking single file past the sarcophagus sitting just outside the entrance.

"Jesus uses humor to teach, heal, convert and, ultimately, redeem. And he does this while modeling the fact that laughter and profundity are not mutually exclusive. The humor of Jesus is subtle, nearly imperceptible at first glance... Jesus exposes our human foibles not to embarrass or condemn but to illuminate and transform. When we take ourselves too seriously, we commit perhaps humanity's greatest sin: trusting in ourselves rather than God. Jesus shows us the absurd consequences that invariably result."[40]

I distinctly felt my Guardian Lord, as I still thought of him then, had been teasing me, and that the subject of this lighthearted parody of a New Kingdom burial ceremony was my continued bondage to ancient Egypt. I now see the cheetah jumping onto the seat beside me as an obvious reference to the fictional biography of the female pharaoh, Hathsepsut-Maatkare, I had recently published, *Truth is the Soul of the Sun*.[41] In my novel, Hatshepsut owns a beloved pet Cheetah. My Lord was clearly pleased with me—he had kissed me twice!—and I did not feel He was condemning me, only that He was telling me something important. It seems to me now that He orchestrated this playful reenactment of a burial ceremony for my benefit, to let me know a part of me was about to die, an old way of thinking and feeling; my obsession with ancient Egypt would soon be laid to rest. I feel the Holy Spirit wanted me to understand that I had recognized Him from the moment I saw Him in my dreams not because He reminded me of an ancient Egyptian pharaoh, but because He is, indeed, King, not of a dead civilization but of all Creation. Yet the way He smiled at me during this ancient Egyptian-style procession of treasures also seemed to be reassuring me that, in some respects at least, He was pleased with my story of Maatkare, whose name means the *True and Beautiful Manifestation of the Sun's Divine Life Force.*

Maatkare's devotion to Amun-Re was deeply spiritual, and her twenty-two year reign was characterized by wisdom and compassion. Art, architecture and religion achieved new heights of inspired beauty, and her people flourished as she rooted out corruption while maintaining and establishing peaceful, mutually profitable relationships with neighboring countries. If you did not know the source of the following prayer, you might never guess it was written by the Old Kingdom pharaoh Merikare, True of Voice:

> "People, the flock of the god, are provided for!
> "He has made the sky and the earth for their heart!
> "He has made the heart's air so that they may live when they breathe!
> "They are his likenesses, who came from his body!
> "He rises in the sky for their hearts!
> "He has made for them the plants, flocks and fish that feed them!
> "He makes sunlight for their hearts and sails across the sky to see them!

> "He has raised a shrine about them; when they weep he is hearing...
>
> "The god knows every name!"[42]

Contrary to popular misconceptions, the great pyramids were not built by Jewish slaves; the Tribe of Abraham did not exist when the pyramids were constructed. It was thousands of years later that the Jewish people were enslaved in Egypt. I believe that, for a time in ancient Egypt, the Spirit of Truth flourished and that God preserved it through Moses, who was raised from infancy as an Egyptian Prince. Ancient Egypt weaves itself into the Bible through the story of Joseph and the power of dreams. As a little girl, it pleased me to learn that Jesus had spent the first seven years of His life in Egypt, which had given him refuge.

> ...That night Joseph left for Egypt with the child and Mary, his mother, and they stayed there until Herod's death. This fulfilled what the Lord had spoken through the prophet: "I called my Son out of Egypt." Matthew 2:14-15[43]

God has been with us from the beginning of Time. Like Moses, I came to the God of the Hebrews through Egypt. In a sense, my soul has made a similar journey. The excessive pride and self-reliance of Pharaoh had to die inside me, but Maatkare's passionate devotion to Amun-Re had spoken to my heart, and as I wrote about her, expressing myself through her, I feel God heard me crying out to Him:

"My Divine mind is looking out for posterity, my king's heart has thought of eternal continuity because of the utterance of Him who parts the ished-tree, Amun. I have magnified the Order He has desired, for it is known to me that He lives in my bread and it is His dew I drink. I was in one body with Him, and He has brought me up to make the awe of Him powerful throughout the land.[44] I never neglect to obey my Father's orders, which are all accomplished according to my prescriptions, and never will I transgress against what my mouth says on this subject. Amun-Re has opened a place in His heart for me who knows all He loves, and what He loves He takes hold of."[45]

The one element of the dream I could not make sense of were the initials **F C** which my Lord pointed out to me at the top of the manuscript I would be working on with Him. Even though in the dream I understood what they meant, when I woke up, I had no clue.

While writing this book, I finally ventured to do a web search for "Christ FC". Apart from endless hits for "Fellowship of Christ" one of the top search results was the Catholic Encyclopedia of ecclesiastical abbreviations that contains the entry F.C., Fieri Curavit, which is Latin for "Cause to be made." I feel the Holy Spirit is causing this book to be made, that we are mysteriously collaborating on it through my dreams, and any errors or misinterpretations arise from the human side of that collaboration.

It is very much worth noting that the week I was working on this chapter, my dream partner, Sean, when trying to find me in a lucid dream, had the following experience:

> "I searched for Maria, and while doing so, I found myself going toward a mountain, getting drawn toward it. This was great. The location we had only just established as our base of operations was already becoming a natural place to go, as happened with Maria yesterday. So I called out Maria's name, and saw something written on the sky—the initials **F C** followed by a dash or another symbol. These were written with the clouds themselves. I had the feeling that someone had put them there specifically."[46]

The Bread of Life

Dream of September 14, 2013

I'm sitting at a wooden table in a large, atmospherically lit room. There are two or three amorphous women sitting across from me, but the tabletop is broad enough that they don't intrude on my personal space. I'm conscious of feeling very tired, not up to preparing my own meal, when I suddenly become aware of a man in an elegant black suit standing very close to me on my left. Smiling down at me, He begins preparing me something to eat. I watch as He works, swiftly but precisely assembling what looks like a delectable sandwich, healthy, satisfying and delicious. I become more and more lucidly aware of Him, until I simply can't resist asking Him, "Will you marry me?!"

He turns his head away from me for a moment, but not before I see his smile deepen. Looking at me again, He quietly tells me there is about "this" much chance of that happening, and before my eyes flashes an image of an eyedropper filled with a luminous gold-orange substance like distilled sunlight.

He presents me with the sandwich, and smiling over his shoulder at me, begins walking away. I distinctly sense He would not have done this for me if He did not feel about me the way I feel about Him. I *know* deep in my heart He feels as I do—we are meant for each other—and that before too long, He will begin courting me in earnest.

Following Him with my eyes as he walks away, I declare to the women sitting across from me, "I'm going to hold *on* to *Him*!"

Grinning, they reply in some typical female fashion, and I wonder if it was a good idea to state my feelings so publicly so soon, but I couldn't stop myself. I *love* this Man, and we *are* going to be together soon, we *have* to be. Treasuring the promise I feel His looks and actions made me, I begin eating the delicious meal He prepared for me.

For the rest of the night, in all my other dreams, I keep remembering, confused, this blonde man I love just as much as the darkly tanned man I first saw lying in a stone tomb. How can this be? How can I feel exactly the same way about two different Guides? Am I only imagining the reality of my relationship with one truly special Guardian Lord? Are these merely dreams with no substance? Then, out of nowhere, a male Voice says very precisely, "He is a negative."

That morning I wrote: In a photographic negative, light registers as darkness. My dark-skinned, and my fair Guardian Lord, are actually one and the same. It is an immense relief to finally understand that this very special blonde Guide is also my original Guardian Lord, which means He has come to me in dreams more often than I realized. And tonight He served me food He prepared for me with His own hands!

> "Sir," they said: "give us that bread everyday." Jesus replied: "I am the bread of life. Whoever comes to me will never be hungry again. Whoever believes in me will never be thirsty. But you haven't believed in me even though you have seen me. However, those the Father has given me will come to me, and I will never reject them." John 6:34-37[47]

I was too tired to feed myself—I was exhausted from clinging to the illusion of self-reliance. When I asked Him, "Will you marry me?" He showed me an eyedropper filled with the light of the Sun, and told me there was *this* much chance of it happening. Little by little, dream by dream, the eyes of my soul were opening to the Light of the World.

Jesus spoke to the people once more and said: "I am the

light of the world. If you follow me, you won't have to walk in darkness, because you will have the light that leads to life." John 8:12[48]

Be dressed for service and keep your lamps burning, as though you were waiting for your master to return from the wedding feast. Then you will be ready to open the door and let him in the moment he arrives and knocks. The servants who are ready and waiting for his return will be rewarded. I tell you the truth, he himself will seat them, put on an apron, and serve them as they sit and eat! He may come in the middle of the night or just before dawn. But whenever he comes, he will reward the servants who are ready." Luke 12:35-38[49]

The Holy Spirit

Dream of November 15, 2013

For the third time, I dream of getting up in the middle of the night in order to move to the Den, where my lucid dreaming bed is.[50] The house looks just as it actually does, and I'm convinced I'm awake. I collect my two pillows along with my iPod, but then pause on my way down the hall to turn the light off in that other (*not real*) bedroom where I dreamed about my two earlier Wake Back To Bed attempts. However, the light in this room will not turn off completely; the circular lamp on the ceiling keeps glowing faintly, like a tiny electrical moon.

With a mental shrug, I continue to the Den. One of the glass doors is open, and I become aware of a strong wind blowing outside. The room is lit as if by bright moonlight, and I feel intensely alive, incredibly excited to be here. There is a white blanket bunched up at the foot of the mattress I don't recognize, but it feels intricately woven and of very soft, fine quality. The invigorating wind is blowing directly over the bed, across which are strewn some light-brown seeds, the kind that twirl through the air like tiny propellers. Everything feels absolutely real, yet also magical...

I wake abruptly, and am amazed I haven't really gotten up yet. This time I actually do so, and move to the bed in the Den, where I soon fall asleep again...

My brother is in the house, and together we proceed to the dark Den, where I sit down in the place where my lucid dreaming bed is in reality. He leaves the room to fetch his camera from my study, and as I wait for him to return, I look out the Bay Windows. In the darkness outside, I can just make out snow falling, the flakes blowing east to west in a strong wind. I think—Oh nice, the first snowfall of the year! As I continue to wait for my brother, I distinctly hear my mother's voice talking. Mami is definitely in the house. I get up, open the Den doors, and my mother walks right in. The room is suddenly well lit in a soft, realistic way, as though she brought the light with her. She's wearing a pretty, ankle-length blue-green nightgown, and she has that ageless young look about her she usually does in my dreams. Still talking, she sits down close to the Bay Windows.

Looking at her intently, I realize out loud, "Mami, you know you're actually asleep and dreaming. You're not really here. This is a dream. We're in a dream." I can tell from her expression that she understands what I'm telling her, but after a moment of considering the possibility, she says, "No, it can't be. I don't remember going to bed."

I know what she means—she doesn't have a realistic sense of continuity, of having been doing something before finding herself here. I say, "That happens to all of us. We don't have a sense of a break in the linear flow of our life, which is why so few people ever wake up in their dreams and realize they're dreaming." (*The sense of my words seems to be that we believe time is linear, and one action follows another in a chain, when in reality it doesn't.*)

I continue trying to convince her, "You actually *did* go to sleep, and this is a dream. Come on, Mami, remember when you wake up that it was 3:30 in the morning, and you were just at Maria's house in a dream..." I am increasingly aware of the wind blowing even more strongly outside. Glancing out the Bay Windows, I see a pair of black tree branches lying across the driveway. In waking reality this might be cause for concern, but in a dream the powerful wind is purely exhilarating. Watching the snow blowing past the windows like an endless white veil, I open my arms wide and let out a cry of sheer exultation that harmonizes with the keening of the wind outside. I *am* the storm! I *am* this magical wind! It is an absolutely marvelous experience to be fully awake and alive in a dream!

Suddenly, I see my maternal grandfather quickly walking out

of the Den into the living room. Dressed all in black, he is as thin and elegant as he was in reality. I declare, "And Abuelo is dreaming with us too!" as I follow him into the living room. "Abuelito?" I call, and although he seems to hear me, I perceive he is not as lucid as Mami. Then I notice the front door is half open, and that a tall Christmas tree is growing just outside it. Decorated with shining red and gold balls, the tree looks as though it is actually part of the door. It is a perfectly lovely Christmas tree, but I feel I should close the door to prevent snow from blowing into the room, and perhaps a bear from wandering inside...

I am sitting in the dark Den across from the glass doors against which my lucid dreaming bed should be, but instead there is a sort of couch directly across from me, occupied by the unclothed figure of a man I can just barely see. He bends his head and, in a flash, I perceive his skull, which resembles a speckled egg. Seeing it is indistinguishable from knowing, from viscerally feeling/grasping/understanding, that his skull is also my skull, because we are One! I remember what I read somewhere "*It will come to you as a revelation*" because it just has! The figure raises his head, and I glimpse my husband's features, but at the same time, I know it could be anyone's face. The "egg" of his head is also my head, we are the same thing split in two, split into endless trillions, yet there is no difference between us. This single "egg" can wear countless faces, but there is only one Life, one miraculously sentient Being...

I am a disembodied awareness watching a film I myself am

shooting, or have already shot, in which I am also acting. I am showing the film to what I sense is a male Presence on my left. In the current scene, I am wearing a long, narrow black dress with an old-fashioned bodice that is cut so low, not only the swells of my breasts but also my nipples are visible. As the camera pans in from right to left, the viewer gets a clear look at my neck, chest and breasts. I am facing a female, also wearing a black dress, who is at the threshold of girlhood and womanhood. As part of a ritual or rite of passage, I give her something to drink while a disembodied voice talks about the tragedy of our children being obliged to drink the evils of the world. The camera focuses on the young woman's face as she swallows the bitter elixir, her facial expressions very dramatic. She has been given poison, yet I know it does not have to—will not at this point in some mysterious process—kill her.

The scene in my dream film changes. The camera lens and hence the observer, who is only me at the moment, is now flush to the white border of a moonlit pool shimmering just outside the glass doors of the Den. My perspective akin to having my face pressed right up against the bottom of the glass door. I watch myself step out of the circular pool directly in front of me, and think—Oh God, I'm actually exposing my naked fifty-two-year-old body so everyone can get a clear view of all its flaws!

As I rise up out of the water, I move gracefully and swiftly counter clockwise along the pool's white border. It is definitely me, yet I don't perceive any of the signs of aging I expected, and dreaded. In one seamless motion, I rise from the pool's dark water, walk a complete circle around the white stone border, and bend down to kiss myself on the lips! Wow! As she keeps her mouth on mine, I study her breasts and figure, appreciating the fact that she/me is slender and flawless in an ageless way. She/me looks like my dream body merged with my physical body, her/my skin a healthy, living color beneath her/my flowing moon-white hair. The experience of being kissed by myself is incredible. Even though I am observing her, I *am* her, and she is me. She/me straightens up, smiling down at me...

I believe I wake up lying in my lucid dreaming bed. Mami is sitting on a green couch at the foot of the bed, and I sense she has been here for a long time, observing me. She says, "I'm so tired" and I realize she's been watching over me as I dreamed. I'm glad she's here, but feel bad that I kept her up. "Go to sleep now," I urge, and as she begins trying to get comfortable on the couch, I say, "Come and sleep on the bed with me." I move over to the left, and as she puts her book and pen down on a nightstand, preparing to slip under the covers with me, I wake for real.

The next day, I emailed Mami my dream, and she responded:

> A few days ago, in the *Raven* bookstore, I bought for less than $3 dollars, a volume of all the paintings of the Sienese school that are in the Metropolitan Museum of New York. And that iconic image of Segna di Buonaventura, who lived during the first part of the XIV Century, "Christ Blessing", struck me as a good

semblance of Stinger. Then, when I got to this part of your dream: *"I remember what I read somewhere "It will come to you as a revelation" because it just has! The figure raises his head, and I see my husband's features, but at the same time I know it could be anyone's face"* I also remembered a line from the Gospel of John: "For God loved the world so much that he gave his one and only Son, so that everyone who believes in him will not perish but have eternal life."[51] He is the One you saw behind the mirage.

The image of Christ Mami emailed me really does resemble my husband, but it looks even more like the face I saw in my dream. I feel my mother was a messenger of Christ; she entered my dream space, bringing the light with her, and remained with me all night.

I knew, in my dream, that I was experiencing a revelation. I know now that the wind blowing around the house of my self was the Holy Spirit. I saw a Christmas tree just outside the front door, a dream image I see as expressing how I had put my Christian upbringing outside of my present way of thinking, but it was still there in my heart, still part of me, just as the tree was part of the house. It was my mother's father who led me into the living room, and this vision of a Christmas tree. I often recall how at his wife's funeral, Abuelito looked earnestly into my eyes and said to me in English, which he rarely spoke, "You just have to faith, Mari. You just have to have faith."

At the time I had this dream, I was flirting with the idea that the bear was my spirit animal. It seemed everywhere I turned, lucid dreamers were talking about their experiences in shamanic terms, and I was, albeit very reluctantly, considering learning more about this perspective myself. But in my dream, I didn't *want* to let the bear in, and it was the Christmas tree which was part of my home, part of my soul. After this incredible night, I began detaching myself from pagan systems of thought. It was becoming increasingly apparent that Christian mysticism was my soul's true path.

The young woman I stood facing—who was forced to drink the evils of the world—I feel embodied my mortal self and personality.

> "In one seamless motion, I rise from the pool's dark water, walk a complete circle around the white stone border, and bend down to kiss myself on the lips... Even though I am observing her, I am her, and she is me."

It was an incredible experience to watch what I felt to be my soul rising up out of the Water of Life, and literally coming full circle to kiss my self. I feel now that this was the moment I finally let go of the futile vanity of self reliance as, through the power of the Holy Spirit, I was born again from above.

> Jesus replied, "I assure you, no one can enter the Kingdom of God without being born of water and the Spirit.* Humans can reproduce only human life, but the Holy Spirit gives birth to spiritual life. So do not be

surprised when I say, 'You must be born again.'

John 3:5-7[52] *The Greek *Spirit* can also be translated *Wind.*

Chapter Eight – Buried Treasure

All that remains as this life
time slowly ebbs away
is the joy of marveling
at the mysteries of God
knowing we can never
touch bottom as the cup
of our soul will be forever
overflowing God in God and us
universes sparkling on the surface
of the unfathomable depths of God

Mary and Elizabeth

Dream of November 18, 2013

The night begins with people deliberately jumping into a river to cross the border, and floating away. I am one of them. It feels disturbingly real to be just one anonymous body drifting slowly along with the current. Sometimes, I even sense fish bumping against my legs, because the water is deep. Where we came from is so terrible, even though we know we will encounter enemies along the shores, it is still better than remaining where we were...

The next thing I know, I'm on a boat, and my two female friends have fallen overboard as the result of some conflict. I desperately strive to save them, but they have already taken the form of two bright orange fish... I enter my grandparents' old bedroom, turn on the light, and am astonished to see them sleeping there just as in my childhood...

The theme of a terrible dystopian society continues. People live squeezed together in refugee camps, where they are supposedly safe, but the military groups in charge have spies on the inside who conspire to have individuals secretly disposed of on a regular basis because of a shortage of food and other supplies. I fight with the Resistance, running through the night alongside my teammates...

When I wake up, I feel very tired, not inspired to move to the Den and my lucid dreaming bed, but I do so anyway.

I'm leaning on a windowsill, looking into a room where sits a young woman with lustrous black hair. She is wearing a long purple-blue tunic, with a sash of a similar vibrant color. She is beautiful, and her aura is utterly peaceful. Beside her stands another woman I know is related to her, and I clearly see her light-brown eyes as they gaze into mine, as well as her coarse brown hair above an ancient-style tunic.

The two women make me think of the Biblical Mary and Elizabeth. They desire to show me something, so I follow them down a set of steps into a dark corridor that turns sharply clockwise. There I pause, gazing through a wall at their luminous figures as they tell me about an egg-shaped hole in this wall. Looking through it, I perceive something like a cellar filled with personal treasures. The space looks neglected, as though it hasn't been accessed for a long time, yet all the furnishings are still there. I open the door to enter, but discover a stone wall blocking my path that frightens me, because this wall *shouldn't* be here.

> "Catherine of Siena puts forward Christ Crucified as a bridge. It is seen 'horizontally' as getting us across a river, saving us from being swept away in its powerful current and it is also seen 'vertically' as connecting earth and heaven. As we journey through life with Christ we also journey towards Heaven. In both cases Christ Crucified rescues us from the river which is understood as sin and even life in hell... Thus encountering Christ at his feet is what we do when we turn from sin, or, in her imagery, pull ourselves out of the river of sin."[53]

My dream reflects the terrible state of the world today, not a future dystopian society. Thousands of people, displaced by wars, are forced to live crowded together in refugee camps, while more and more immigrants are crossing borders in a desperate effort to escape hellish regimes, and crippling poverty.

Seeing my grandparents sleeping peacefully together in their old bedroom was such a bittersweet experience! I felt as though I had literally gone back in time to my childhood. My two female friends who fell out of the boat—whereupon they immediately transformed into orange fish—strike me now as a reference to the young nuns who drowned in a freak storm one day while I was an infant, and my mother and I were taking refuge in their convent. Growing up, I often thought of them, especially about the one who rocked me vigorously in her arms every night, for otherwise I refused to fall sleep. I always felt these sisters' souls were mysteriously linked with mine, and felt deeply sad their lives—which briefly but intimately converged with mine—had been cut short so abruptly. Vaguely, uneasily, I wondered what kind of omen this was about my own future. But in my dream, the two women who fell out of the boat immediately swam away as beautiful bright fish. In reality, *I* am the one who, for decades, struggled in the potentially soul-drowning currents of the world, adrift in the river of sin. I feel now there was a profound reason I spent the first few months of my life sheltered, and cherished, in a house dedicated to God's Mother. I see it now as a promise that, even though I would come perilously close to drowning in doubts and fears, I would at last come home to the faith that protects all of us from evil.

I was blessed with the chance to regain something I might have lost forever—the undying security that makes me feel like a child again, safe at home where I am loved unconditionally. The exile my confused, arrogant, sinful self imposed on my soul has ended, I have come home to the faith I felt when I was young, home to my family, part of a greater family—the family of Christ, my soul a little child sitting at the feet of her loving Father, who she trusts to always cherish and protect her.

> "About that time the disciples came to Jesus and asked, "Who is the greatest in the Kingdom of Heaven?" Jesus called a little child to him and put the child among them. Then he said, "I tell you the truth, unless you turn

from your sins and become like little children, you will never get into the Kingdom of Heaven. So anyone who becomes as humble as this little child is the greatest in the Kingdom of Heaven." Matthew 18:1-3[54]

Mary and Elizabeth led me down a set of steps I was taking deeper through my self into my soul. All the spiritual treasures I was heir to were still there, waiting for me to rediscover them.

The Battle

Dream of November 22, 2013

My sister is urgently calling our mother on a black phone while I watch and listen. We are crouching in the open door of a large building akin to a barn or a stable. It's daytime, and we're looking out at an open expanse of packed dirt, around the edges of which, in a rough horseshoe shape, sprawls an old town. I don't know the whole story, but I fervently agree with my sister as she speaks urgently into the phone, saying, "Mami, please come home! They're intending to practice black magic against you! You're in danger!"

Even as we're warning our mother, a man walks across the open space toward us. Stopping a few feet away, he stares at me with undisguised anger and hostility. Looking back at him, I become semi-lucid as I plan to keep him away from us with an invisible force-field. But already his partners in crime are lining up to his right, and now there is a group of hostile men facing me.

I rise from my crouching position to confront them, yet as I begin raising my right hand, intending to project a defensive force against their leader, I abort the gesture. Instead, I stride fearlessly toward them, and opening my arms wide declare in a voice that carries through the town, "My brothers! I welcome you in love!" I am intensely conscious of being filled with the invulnerable light of the Holy Spirit, with the love and compassion of Christ, as the line of men slowly backs away from me. I don't remember everything I say to them, but moving forward as they continue to retreat, I notice birds being drawn to the confrontation—large black birds like vultures coming to rest on the roofs of the surrounding buildings.

My ringing voice effortlessly reaches a crowd of people, who have also gathered to watch, as I cry, "Why do you do this when eternal life is yours, freely given? You need no magic or spells! Life eternal is yours already by the grace of God! Why do you turn against your Father? It is as foolish as little children turning against their father!"

The man who had first approached me retreats into a single-story building, and when the man closest to him turns his head in that direction, I quickly step up to him. As he glances back at me, I draw a short bright-green line on his right cheek. Then I back away and, smiling, say, "Fire burns." Immediately, a flame burns across his cheek. At this point, the man cowering in the dark building sends two floating spheres out toward me, one slightly bigger than the other. They look like models of the earth and the moon, and as they drift closer, I know they are filled with a poisonous energy that will attack me. I raise my right hand, with my palm held up, and the spheres simply dissolve, falling in a soft rain of ashes to the ground. Slowly, I wake.

I still remember how astonished I was by my actions in this dream, and by everything I said. The words welled up from within me, as did the precise authority with which I spoke them; I didn't need to think about them, I simply knew, beyond a shadow of a doubt, that everything I said was true.

> The rule was laid down by the apostle Paul when he wrote, "But as then he that was born after the flesh persecuted him that was born after the Spirit, even so it is now." Differences of moral standards between the once-born and the twice-born, and their opposite ways of life, may be contributing causes of this hostility; but the real cause lies deeper. There are two spirits abroad in the earth: the spirit that works in the children of disobedience and the Spirit of God... The spirit that dwells in the once-born is forever opposed to the Spirit that inhabits the heart of the twice-born.[55]

The life of the once-born revolves around the pleasures and concerns of the physical world just as the moon, trapped in its orbit, revolves around the earth, but it is a dead existence, and in the end all that is left is ashes.

Modern Christians may understandably have little

knowledge of or taste for the angelology or demonology of the early church, but this does not excuse them from grasping how radically the gospel is pervaded by a sense that the brokenness of the fallen world is the work of rebellious rational free will, which God permits its reign, and pervaded also by a sense that Christ comes genuinely to *save* creation, to conquer, to rescue, to defeat the power of evil in all things. This great narrative of fall and redemption is... a real consequence of the mystery of created freedom and the fullness of grace.[56]

Angels Sing

Dream of December 17, 2013

I am part of a small crowd of people standing outside on a sunny winter day. The atmosphere feels very festive, and we are all watching a most incredible performance. Before me, and slightly to my left, approximately six "men" are floating side-by-side a few feet above the street. They are singing as they dart back and forth along a straight line, constantly changing places and returning to their original positions with the energetic precision of humming birds. They are all wearing what I can only describe as Christmas uniforms, red form-fitting jackets and pants with gold trim.

I don't recall any words now, but in the dream their singing is the unclouded sound of pure joy, their united voices ringing with the clarity and resonance of a great bell. The complexions of the singers is almost luminous, and everything about the scene is so perfect, I remark to one of my female companions that it reminds me of an old Hollywood musical's slightly unreal Technicolor. But then I quickly add, "I know who they are, they are angels of the Divine assuming human form simply for the joy of self expression!"

Abruptly, one of the singers zooms in on our semi-circle of female bodies muffled in dark coats. As he hovers just above and outside our group, I cannot resist the desire to speak to him, and to ask him, "What are you?" Immediately, I wish I could take my question back, because now he will be forced to reply in front of everyone, and that wouldn't be right.

He does not answer me, but instead offers us the opportunity to touch him. Or perhaps the opposite occurs, and he asks permission to touch one of us. The point is, *touch* is the purpose here. We are all more than willing, and when he zooms directly in on me, I feel immensely honored. He seems to know I want to kiss him, and he apparently wants to kiss me as well, because when I don't dare move any closer, he presses his mouth against mine. His firm lips are chastely puckered, and his pale face is so very close to mine, it takes up my entire field of vision, like a patch of moonlit sky framed by darkness. His mouth, which almost feel carved of wood, remains firmly pressed against mine for a long moment as his open eyes study my reaction.

Then, our faces still as close as they can be, he begins speaking to me very quietly. In the dream, I can just barely hear and understand what he says, but I can't remember any of it now. He abruptly ends the long explanation of his nature by telling me his name, "Harim." This really surprises me, and I echo, "Harim?" but he only smiles at me, and I lose the dream.

That morning I wrote: I had no idea what to make of the name Harim so I did a web search for "Angel" and "Harim" and discovered that Harim is an ancient Hebrew name which means "Consecrated to God." It is pronounced Haw-reem, how I heard it spoken in my dream.[57]

Christmas Is Coming

Dream of January 10, 2014

I find myself outside on a clear sunny day, and immediately know I'm dreaming. I turn in place, and perceive that I'm alone somewhere very up high, graced with a breathtaking view of distant mountains. At first, I think I'm close to my waking reality home, but as I follow a smooth dirt path, winding in the direction of the far away mountain chain, I take note of the fact that the steep slopes are a golden-brown color, arid looking, and with sharper peaks. Am I perhaps farther west? Then I wonder if I'm not actually inside a massive film studio, because the spectacular view looks almost like a painted mural. The path hugs one side of the mountain, which looms on my right. To my left, there appears to be another huge, totally realistic mural depicting a flat area overlooking a valley far below. This curious phenomena quenches any desire I might have to simply fly away, and instead I call out playfully, hopefully, "Is one of my Guides around here somewhere?"

In keeping with the Hollywood set-like aura of the scene, I skip down the gradually descending path while singing, "I'm off to see the Wizard, the wonderful Wizard of Oz!"

Suddenly, as I round a sharp curve in the path before me, I come upon a completely unexpected sight—a thin, dark-skinned version of Santa Claus leading a big beautiful elephant hauling some sort of cart. The gray elephant's forehead, and the space between its eyes, is covered by the off-white material of its harness. I think—Wow! and approach the incongruous pair. His face brown and wrinkled as a walnut shell, Santa smiles at me benignly as I curiously study the glass bottles of assorted fruit juices, which appear to be the sole contents of his cart. I don't remember if Santa says anything to me, but before I move on, I attempt to high-five the gentle, lovely elephant by placing my hand on its forehead, and in return its eyes smile into mine.

Following the mountain path, I don't remember a transition as I end up in what feels like a partially open-air market only pleasantly crowded with people. A male vendor, a nice looking man of middle years, catches my eye, and encourages me to look at the glass bottles lined up in a long metal cooler beside him. They all appear to be bottles of fruit juice, and I say, "Okay, I get it, I should drink more fruit juices. But won't they make me gain weight?"

He assures me they won't, then grins at me and says, "Merry Christmas! Christmas is coming, and it's coming for you in eighty-two days."

I feel he's telling me that something wonderful, something very special, is coming my way, something which is going to make me incredibly happy.

Turning around, I find myself descending a set of steps, but I deliberately climb back up, not wanting to get trapped inside somewhere. Wondering what I should do next, I head toward what looks like the exit to this pleasant market-mall. A glass door leads out onto a sunny city sidewalk, where I immediately notice a large bird gliding approximately six or seven feet above the ground. The creature captures my entire attention, because it is not a real bird; it is made of cloth, and resembles an elaborate oversized theater prop. It is a beautiful dark-blue color with gold-tipped feathers, and when I hail it by raising my right arm, it flies right up to my fingertips, where it hovers obediently. It has a turkey-shaped body, a slender curved neck, a short and sharp, slightly curved beak, and yellow-gold eyes that actually seem to look back into mine. I experienced a feeling of deja vu when I first caught sight of it; we somehow know each other.

When this mysteriously animated cloth bird follows me across the street, I spontaneously tell it, "I love you!"

Spreading it's short wings, it replies, "I love you too."

Pleased and surprised that it spoke, I ask, "You do?" but my question is rhetorical, for I can *feel* that it loves me.

As we pass what looks like a fine hotel, I decide I want to experience the physical pleasure of a dream massage. Turning toward a low wall, I ask my bird friend to help hoist me up onto a ledge leading into what appears to be a beauty salon, where I immediately plan to find a spa on the floor above it. I know I risk waking up during the experience of a massage, but I'm willing to try it. As I walk in the direction of steps I intend on being there, a woman says something about the water always being hot enough to keep the germs alive, apparently referring sarcastically to the spa's hot tub in an effort to spoil my pleasant anticipation. I reply, "I'm in my dream body, so I don't care." Upstairs, there is indeed a massage center.

I begin removing my clothes in a shadowy room, letting the attendant know I would prefer a female therapist. But when a young man walks into the room, and then departs again carrying some towels, I change my mind and decide it would be more stimulating for a man to massage me. I slowly wake.

Because I had this dream in January, shortly after Christmas, I reasoned that I was simply feeling nostalgic for this most special of holidays. The number "eighty-two" was more of an enigma, perhaps symbolic of something, because obviously Christmas wasn't literally coming again in April. Yet precisely eighty-two days later, just as the man who drew my attention to a cooler of fruit juices promised it would, Christmas did indeed come for me in the dream that transformed my life.

I can well understand now the meaning of all those bottles of assorted fruit juices—the fruits of the Spirit—as well as the final part of the dream, where I succumbed to the temptation of being massaged by a handsome young stranger.

> "Galatians 5:22-23 tells us, "But the fruit of the Spirit is love, joy, peace, patience, kindness, goodness, faithfulness, gentleness and self-control." The fruit of the Holy Spirit is the result of the Holy Spirit's presence in the life of a Christian. The Bible makes it clear that everyone receives the Holy Spirit the moment he or she believes in Jesus Christ (Romans 8:9; 1 Corinthians 12:13; Ephesians 1:13-14). One of the primary purposes of the Holy Spirit coming into a Christian's life is to change that life. It is the Holy Spirit's job to conform us to the image of Christ, making us more like Him... Our sinful flesh produces certain types of fruit that reflect our nature, and the Holy Spirit produces types of fruit that reflect His nature... the new nature given by Christ (2 Corinthians 5:17).[58]

I feel my longing to come home to Christianity was expressed in this dream.

Chapter Nine – The King's Chamber

In universes born of Love
my soul longs to shine
burning in service to God
sands of atoms divinely blown
into tiny mirrors of the I AM
my creative mind experiencing
my soul delighting in imagining
Truth desires to live within me
space and time my heart beating

Talking to my Lord About Lucid Dreaming

Dream of February 10, 2014 (*The morning after my birthday*)

I'm busy eating rice and eggs at a table, when I abruptly remember I forgot the leftover meatloaf I'm warming up in the oven. Silly me! I pull it out, and see it's already sliced. At that moment, I become aware of my beloved Guardian Lord walking by. I get the impression He is on his way home after a long day. Without hesitation, I boldly ask Him if He would like to rest a moment and have some home-made meatloaf, "Hot out of the oven!" I declare. He does not hesitate, but readily accepts my invitation. I sit down again, so that I am partially across from and beside Him. He is very close, and it is wonderful having Him here eating food I have prepared, His eyes on me as he listens attentively to what I have to say.

"I've dreamed about you before," I tell him. "Are you familiar with lucid dreaming?"

He replies, "Oh yes" in a way that encourages me to go on. I feel He already knows what I'm getting at; I feel He knows about our ongoing relationship in the dream space.

I say, "All my life I've had spontaneous lucid dreams, but I called them 'flying dreams' because that's immediately what I would do since it felt so good. It wasn't until I read Robert Waggoner's book[59] that I began consciously lucid dreaming, and having anywhere from three to five lucid dreams a month." He listens attentively the whole time, and I tell Him about my lucid dreaming Blog. There is no doubt He is interested in the subject, and after years of seeing Him on and off in dreams, it is glorious to finally be talking about our dream space relationship.

After a time, He gets up to leave. Where we are now resembles a shadowy restaurant-pub, the heart of which is a large circular bar, and it is beginning to fill with people. One of these persons is my late grandmother, who I also frequently see in dreams, and who looks astonished such an important Man is associating so intimately with me. I know what most people don't realize—that every single night my beloved Guardian Lord passes me on His way home. He and I are well acquainted, and I often have the opportunity to exchange a few words with Him. But tonight is significant, for He actually stayed to eat with me. It feels perfectly natural that He accepted my invitation, and yet it is still incredibly special, and I feel very happy.

My Lord passes close by me again on His way to a smaller,

private bar set in the dark wall. He informs the man behind the counter that all drinks for everyone are on Him. The bartender looks nonplussed, because this is not proper protocol, but my Lord insists, and I find myself covering my mouth with my hand as I laugh in delight at some of the things he says, occasionally smiling my way. I feel like the center of His attention, and wonder at my good fortune. Yet I know the reason I am able to attract him is because he has the power to see who I am inside.

My Lord then tells the bartender the troops are to be treated to something even more special tonight. Glancing around, I notice a handful of men in uniform at the back of the room, but He is actually referring to a young couple, a woman and her husband, seated together at the main bar. My Lord intends to honor them with a night in a very special place reserved only for the elite. A door opens in the dark wall, and I study the woman's expression of stunned wonder as I see what she does—a bright silvery light suffusing the space beyond. The couple's uncertainty vanishes as they hurry into the luminous space, where I know they will have everything they can possibly desire. My Lord and I are smiling at each other as I wake.

I feel I can read this dream loud and clear now. The drinks are His blood, with which He paid for our sins. The troops are those who believe in Christ and strive to do God's Will, fighting the weakness of their fallen nature, and the forces of evil at work in the world.

I feel my Lord was letting me know in this dream that I was properly nourishing our growing relationship, while offering me a glimpse of the transcendent joy awaiting my soul should I always keep my eyes and heart fixed on Him. When I woke, I was left with the transcendent impression our souls have the power to become the threshold joining heaven and earth if we fully trust in, and open our hearts to, God's love for us.

Breath of Life

Dream of April 2, 2014

I dream I'm in south Florida again, or so I identify this place of sand and palm trees. I realize I live alone in a little white house... I am editing a short film with a historical theme, which I have set to music, and am running through the first shots. The subject is a certain time in history, and I know it's really good. I want to watch the whole thing, but I get up to do something else first...

I'm standing just inside a building, where my beloved Guardian Lord—looking as he did the night He walked into my dream bedroom—has finished holding a press conference or some similar event. Wearing a supremely elegant black suit, He is standing to the right of the open door. He watches me closely as I walk past Him, casually making my way out of the building for a moment with the intention of fetching a camera from my car. I *really* want to take a picture of Him before He leaves, and with a joyful thrill, I sense Him still observing me as I cross the street. His undivided attention makes me so happy, I perform a jaunty little skip-dance beneath the bare branches of a tree as I approach my vehicle, wanting nothing more than for Him to witness my vibrant good nature as I bask in his His pleasure and approval.

Quickly returning to the building, I sit down at my desk to work. The modest-sized room is now my waking reality study. Suddenly, my Lord steps up behind me, and quietly commands me to get up. Surprised and thrilled, I immediately obey Him. He leads me across the room, and makes me stand with my back to a window. He is so close, I distinctly feel his breath as, holding my eyes, He whispers, "I love you."

Not only my heart, but my very soul, seems to stop. I can scarcely believe I heard Him say the words, but I know I didn't imagine them. He is really here with me, and He actually said, "I love you." Then, caressing a stray lock of hair away from my face, he leans down and kisses me on the mouth.

Behind Him, men and women begin entering the room, eager to be with Him, and I suddenly worry He's taking a risk by being so publicly intimate with someone, yet He has eyes only for me as He kisses me again. No one sees Him kiss me, but I'm still a little frightened as He looks directly and intently into my eyes... He loves me! He loves me! Overwhelmed by the joy of our secret love for each other, which He has just undeniably proved to me is real, I wake.

That morning I wrote: This is the first time my beloved

Guardian Lord has ever told me, straight out, in so many words, "I love you." I still can't believe it. In fact, no other dream character of any kind has ever said to me "I love you" in a dream. I searched all my dream journals, and only I myself have said the words "I love you" to someone in a dream.

◐

I could scarcely find the words then to describe how this dream made me feel, *still* makes me feel. I emailed one of my dream partners, passionately attempting to describe the experience to her:

> "You know I have a strong faith in, relationship with, Lucid Guardians. Well, what happened last night felt like a stone in the wall of a castle bedchamber giving way, a keystone opening up a secret passageway into the King's chamber, where I came face to face with the Lord of my Soul, the Life of my breath, the Love of my heart... God's love, in the form of my beloved Guardian Lord, literally backed me up against a wall, breathed on me, and then twice gently kissed me on the lips."

I had never read *The Song of Songs*, only seen select verses quoted here and there. So I felt a confirming joy when someone else I shared this dream with, a fellow Presenter at the 2014 IASD Psiber Dream Conference, sent me this excerpt in response:

> Let him kiss me with the kisses of his mouth—

> for your love is more delightful than wine.
> ...
> Take me away with you—let us hurry!
> Let the king bring me into his chambers.

I knew what had happened to me was much more than just special. I had never experienced anything like this in a dream. I had actually felt His breath on my lips; He had breathed on me, and I had felt both overjoyed and frightened.

> "Then he breathed on them and said, "Receive the Holy Spirit." John 20:22[60]

I have never truly awoken from this dream. When I opened my eyes that morning, my soul was on fire, and it still is. And that fire was stoked to a blaze when I read what A.W. Tozer has to say about the Holy Spirit. If I had read Tozer sooner—but of course I wouldn't have, because he is a Christian writer, and I believed myself to be less than interested in anything he would have to say—I hope I would not have been so blind to what was happening in my dream life. But I never knew I could experience God intimately, in my very soul, as a Person.

> How shall we think of the Holy Spirit? The Bible declares that He is God. Every quality belonging to Almighty God is freely attributed to Him. All that God is, the Spirit is declared to be.

How shall we think of the Holy Spirit? The Bible and Christian theology agree to teach that He is a Person, endowed with every quality of personality, such as emotion, intellect and will. He knows, He wills, He loves; He feels affection, antipathy and compassion. He thinks, sees, hears and speaks and performs any act of which personality is capable... We must never think of Him as a blind energy nor as an impersonal force. He hears and sees and feels as any person does. He speaks and hears us speak. We can please Him or grieve Him or silence Him as we can any other person. He will respond to our timid effort to know Him and will ever meet us over half the way.

One quality belonging to the Holy Spirit, of great interest and importance to every seeking heart, is penetrability. He can penetrate mind; He can penetrate another spirit, such as the human spirit. He can achieve complete penetration of and actual intermingling with the human spirit. He can invade the human heart and make room for Himself without expelling anything essentially human. The integrity of the human personality remains unimpaired. Only moral evil is forced to withdraw.[61]

Reuben Archer writes in *The Person and Work of the Holy Spirit*:

The Holy Spirit is not a blind, impersonal influence or power that comes into our lives to illuminate, sanctify and empower them. No, He is immeasurably more than that, He is a holy Person who comes to dwell in our hearts, One who sees clearly every act we perform, every word we speak, every thought we entertain, even the most fleeting fancy that is allowed to pass through our minds... He is not merely an influence that enables us to see the way that God would have us go, nor merely a power that gives us strength to go that way, but a Person who takes us by the hand and gently leads us on in the paths in which God would have us walk.[62]

In his book *On the Holy Spirit*, Saint Basil wrote that the Holy Spirit is:

An intelligent being, boundless in power, of unlimited greatness, generous in goodness, whom time cannot measure. All things thirsting for holiness turn to Him; everything living in virtue never turns away from Him. He waters them with his life-giving breath and helps them reach their proper fulfillment... He does not increase by additions, but is always complete, self-established, and present everywhere. He is the source of sanctification, spiritual light, who gives illumination to everyone using His power to search for the truth-and the illumination He gives is Himself.

In His Company

Dream of April 4, 2014 (*Precisely 82 days after I was told*

"Christmas is Coming For you in 82 days" in an earlier lucid dream.)

I'm at my place of employment, the sprawling elegant floor of a building that feels like a great highrise. I follow a woman into an empty conference room, where we sit across from each other at the table. Pulling out my file, she leafs through it, and takes notes as she addresses me. This is some kind of performance review, and it's obvious from the start that she isn't pleased with my markedly unprofessional attitude. There's no question about the fact that I do my work, and do it well, what she doesn't like is that I finish too quickly, which gives me time to do what, in her opinion, amounts to nothing useful since it doesn't serve the Company. She says, "And because you have such an ebullient, positive nature, it affects others." Meaning I should make better use of my talents. Then she lays out some kind of form.

Shortly after my meeting with the woman, I walk into a space so large, I can't see where it ends. I sense, more than perceive, it is furnished with intimate little islands, of one or two desks each, scattered throughout it. The lighting is clear and even, but more pleasantly atmospheric than bright. As I approach my desk, I realize that our Boss, accompanied by His special visitor, has left a central area close to where I sit. They have moved to a large spherical room with a glass wall several yards away to my left. I see then that the Boss is my beloved Guardian Lord, just barely visible to me where He sits at his desk facing the open doorway.

To the left of the entrance (from my perspective) sit a row of people at a long table, and I somehow know they are all engrossed in the task of answering questions on a form of some kind. One of these people is my favorite comedian, Stephen Colbert, who appears as he might on a day off, unshaven, his hair loose and natural. He looks incredibly handsome, and studying the relaxed, yet also serious concentration on his face as he fills out some mysterious paperwork, I experience desire, hot, sweet, and indistinguishable from a stab of longing to be seen and desired in return. Body and soul, I surrender to this feeling/sensation, accepting the powerful current of profound attraction, letting it flow through me, permitting it to possess me.

I am about to sit down at my desk when my Lord's distant figure catches my eye. He makes a slight gesture with his right hand, discretely but unmistakably waving me over to Him. I can scarcely describe the relief and joy that floods me when I realize He sees me, and has actually been aware of me the whole time.

Literally feeling how much He wants me near Him, as much as I long to be near Him, I am lucidly conscious of my posture as I walk toward the glass or crystal chamber, quickly but not hastily, my back straight but relaxed. Wearing a black skirt and shirt over knee-high black boots, my dream body is in its prime, my long unbound hair the dark-brown I was born with.

My Lord, clad in His supremely elegant black suit, leaves his desk to meet me at one side of the open entrance. The clear wall, and the row of seated people facing it, are directly to my left. Smiling, He glances over at Colbert and says, "Because of... we were able to... the other night..." Then, looking directly at me, He grips my hips and pulls my lower body against his, casually but forcefully enough for my back to arch as my head is flung gently back. His remark generates some lighthearted laughter as my features press gently against His chest, yet I can still see His face above mine. All that exists for me now is this gloriously intimate darkness which is all about us.

He asks me, speaking softly in Spanish, "Cómo te sientes?" ("How do you feel?")

His loving question, surprisingly spoken in the language of my childhood, makes it impossible for me to find my voice for a moment. I know in my heart He is referring to our dream meeting the other night, where he told me He loved me. I murmur, "Muy bien... gracias a la otra noche." ("Very well... thanks to the other night.")

Smiling, he echoes my response, "Gracias a la otra noche." Our bodies remain intimately pressed against each others as He makes another casual, amusing remark to someone as they walk by. Then, looking only at me again, He asks in the same quiet voice, speaking in English now, "When did we do that?"

I believe he is asking me on exactly what night we dreamed together this week. I can't remember the exact date or day, I only know that it was very recently. Finally, I reply, "Last Saturday night" feeling that I remembered correctly (*it was actually last Monday night*.)

Taking a step back, He tells me, his eyes serious, "I am going to try to–"

Just then my husband loudly closes the bathroom door, and wakes me up!

★ ◐

That morning I emailed Mami my dream, and she replied:

> "That he addressed you in the language of your childhood gives the measure of the intimacy and importance of the communication."

I agreed. For me, Spanish is the language of love, spoken to me from birth by all those I loved. Then a question sprang up in my soul that I dared to ask myself:

Could this beloved Guardian Lord of my dreams be Christ Himself?

"I love you." No one in my dreams had ever spoken those words to me.

In the first dream in which I saw Him, He was lying on a stone bed, his body wrapped in a white shroud, and I knew he was about to rise again... in my heart? Stephen Colbert is a devout Catholic, and his presence in my dream helped to reinforce for me what I suddenly felt I had experienced—the presence of Christ our Lord in my dreams.

Driving home up the mountain the day after this dream, the sun setting on my left, I spoke out loud as I asked God to help me glorify Him through my gift of lucid dreaming.

Just before I woke, my Lord said, "I am going to try to..." I feel He was telling me what I should say to myself, secure in the knowledge He will help me, for through Him I can achieve all my creative intentions as long as they are pleasing to, and serve to glorify, God.

I do not feel the dream was interrupted, I think it ended precisely when the Lord intended, for it has left me with this tantalizing opening, as if what He was about to say depends on my soul's deepening and ever growing relationship with Him.

At the beginning of this dream, I was receiving some kind of performance review. In my mind, this special Company represents Christianity.

Faith

Dream of April 13, 2014

I become aware of sitting on a bench in a large, church-like building. Many of us are gathered here. Someone is speaking. The future is uncertain; the forces of ignorance and evil are rallying. The service is drawing to a close, at which point people begin using their Smart Phones to post messages of love and gratitude on a huge screen above the altar. I write something on mine, a message to my beloved Guardian Lord, but I stop short when I suddenly sense Him sitting directly behind me. Nothing I write can possibly capture how I feel about Him, feelings too profound to mingle with the public tweets flashing across the screen. Then I realize my reticence is linked to pride, with not wanting my intensely special and personal feelings diluted with those of the masses. But it doesn't really matter, because I know *He* knows how I feel about Him.

Yet there is a problem... the massive screen is swiftly

darkening, the words on it becoming illegible, and the reflection of the congregation is also fading. Soon the screen will be completely black. I know it is being sabotaged by the opposing party, but I can only sit there, desperately hoping those in charge will realize what is happening, and do something about it before it's too late.

Just when it seems our enemies will be victorious, I perceive a wondrous sight in the screen's dark-green depths—I see all of us in the congregation floating gently in the air, which has become water and flooded the church. We all rise slowly, and then sink back down again in a slow, peaceful, wave-like rhythm, our bodies, bent at the waists, completely relaxed, our arms and hair hanging limp as the branches of weeping willows. I don't understand what is happening, all I know is that because we are able to behave like fish—because we are of one mind in this Water of Life—evil has no power over us even though it continues to threaten the world as we know it.

I then become aware of a row of men standing on a long pedestal just above the altar, all of them ideally handsome and in the prime of life. When the man on the far right issues an announcement or a command, echoed by the man next to him and continuing down the line, I understand they are preventing our enemies from sabotaging the communal screen above the altar, and that all will be well...

I have left the church, and am on my way home. I am about to walk into a stairwell, when a young black woman appears in the corridor, which is lined with large windows revealing a misty-white day. As she walks up to me, I recognize her from the service at the church. She has come to warn me that I have been spotted and targeted by our enemies, who observed me leaving the church. I suffer a sinking feeling at her words, but cling to the hope she is being overly cautious. After all, I have never been a prominent member of this congregation, never a spokesperson for it, and I protest, "But there were so many people there. Why should our enemies notice me in particular?"

She tells me that she overheard them describing me, and when she repeats what they said, I know it's true: I'm on their list now, and they will most likely target me. Perhaps I came to their attention because I was sitting so close to my Lord. Whatever the reason, I know I have to watch my back.

Slender yet strong looking, her hair a mane of dreadlocks that sway gently as she walks, the woman tells me I need to come with her. She all but commands me to do so; it isn't a request. She leads me to a nearby home, where an important, more exclusive meeting is about to take place. We enter an intimate little dining space adjoining a corridor. The home is humble but clean, and the small table is very nicely appointed, with white place mats and shining white plates. I am led to understand royalty is expected, and despite the mundane setting, this makes sense to me... I phase out of the dream.

That morning I wrote: It occurred to me yesterday that the ancient Egyptian Canopic shrine I believed I saw covered by a shroud-like cloth in a recent lucid dream, *Into Moonlight,*[63] was a sign that I should leave behind mechanical-metaphysics and embrace the purity of Faith. In that same dream, I heard celestial music when I entered a pyramid-shaped pool of moonlight.

I have been seriously thinking that my beloved Guardian Lord may truly be Christ. For years, I have been joyfully drawn to this Man in my dreams. I love Him deeply, more than anyone or anything, and I know He loves me. But even standing so close to Him in my most recent dream, our bodies pressed together, my face at the level of his heart, what I felt was not sexual desire but a great, almost inexpressible joy at finally being in His embrace, and fully experiencing His love for me.

I have always felt my beloved Lord was above me, like a Guide yet *much* more, in charge of everything. In my dreams with Him, the blessing of the powerful love we feel for each other is its own fulfillment. It is not a lucid romance, it is not sexual, it is pure, absolute, unconditional, immutable love. Ever since the dream where He told me He loved me, all I want to do is serve and honor this boundless feeling of love that fills me whenever I think of Him.

I believe the Man in my dreams is my personal experience of Christ! What was between us before—the feeling I had that we couldn't be together—was my own doing, my own reticence, a spiritual political correctness that caused me to perceive all religions as akin to languages, most of which basically state the same things. But only through Christ does God *personally* identify and express Himself as all-powerful Love.

As a little girl, I knew it would be a foolish mistake to confuse

Christ with the church as an institution run by flawed human beings, but as adults we can be influenced too strongly by social pressure and, ashamed of being considered old-fashioned, unimaginative and childish, I hid Christ away deep within myself. Through these series of dreams, I feel my heart has been returned to me, my faith, which gives me permission to love, love, love forever! *"Love, love, love, without love, where would I be?"* I still feel the way I did as a child. The cells in my physical body have died and been replaced, reborn, countless times since then, and who I am will continue transforming, but this feeling of love, of loving, never changes, never dies, never dims, is never forgotten. Even when you grow to dislike someone you once loved, deep down the love is still there, because the Divine power of Love *is* Life, the fundamental, inscrutable heart of Consciousness Itself.

In my dream last night, the ocean was contained in a church, where the congregation floated peacefully as fish out of reach of our enemies. The fish was a sign by which followers of Christ secretly identified themselves to each other in the beginning, when they were being persecuted, as they are being persecuted now, both intellectually and physically. The infinite love and compassion at the heart of the Christian faith has no place in a world ruled by materialistic greed, which has borne the fruit of rampant environmental destruction. Instead of an all-loving Creator God, we take to bed with us every night the heartless ejaculation of the Big Bang, a trivializing label for what remains the unfathomable Power behind Creation.

Chapter Ten – Upheld

It all boils down
to love and disposition –
mine is all for God

Shadows on a wall form
a large pencil of Light
drawing me into the picture

Consciousness can be the gift of knowing
God is my heart and lives in the world
but today's laws are so contrary to love
I suffer a shock in my every thought
caught in selfish wars against the Spirit
taught to mistrust the peace of faith
by vain reason arguing for death

Blessed and challenged by my dreams
I feel embraced by He who is all of me
my sharpening soul the Spirit's pencil
writing these lines in defense of Christ

Martyrs

Dream of May 11, 2014

I find myself walking in daylight alongside a wall that is approximately twice my height, where it has been erected on a mountain meadow. The wall is composed of individual mausoleums, mostly white with some black details, each one topped with a carved effigy of the deceased, both males and females. This mysterious graveyard stretches for miles all around. Then a Voice fills the dream with the words, "The abandonment of Christ."

I am aware of being surrounded by the tombs of great spiritual warriors, who all fought in a battle which has been raging for centuries, and is escalating. I am struck by how different this place is from Arlington cemetery; instead of anonymous crosses, individually unique mausoleums stand side-by-side, so close together, there is truly no space between them. The faith and courage of these souls is forever honored here in this meadow high above the world. I feel they all fought heroically for the Light—for Christ, the Light of the World—and are still mysteriously defending Him.

At the time I had this dream, I was ignorant of how many people are being killed in the world today because of their Christian faith.

> "The most dramatic religion story of the early twenty-first century, yet one that most people in the West have little idea is even happening, (is) the global war on Christians. We're not talking about a metaphorical 'war on religion' in Europe and the United States, fought on

symbolic terrain such as whether it's okay to erect a nativity scene on the courthouse steps, but a rising tide of legal oppression, social harassment, and direct physical violence, with Christians as its leading victims. However counter-intuitive it may seem in light of popular stereotypes of Christianity as a powerful and sometimes oppressive social force, Christians today indisputably form the most persecuted religious body on the planet, and too often its new martyrs suffer in silence."[64]

Light and Shadow

Dream of May 23, 2014

At the tail end of a sequence of dreams, I'm standing in the foyer of a restaurant studying a sign that indicates this is a place where people in relationships, or people looking for relationships, meet up. Two or three women pass behind me, talking. They are self-assured, and searching for someone different who will appreciate them. I'm not really into being here, and as I turn to go, I see that the shadowy pub-like space I envisioned as their meeting place is actually a cheap little diner counter that looks as though it serves only greasy breakfasts. Definitely *not* interested.

I drape a bright white shawl over my shoulders, and it wafts behind me as I step out onto a sidewalk in the early morning hours. I seem to have been wandering through this city all night by myself, exploring on my own, which is different, and good. I am very conscious of my body, and of walking beside a low stone wall on my left that might be the edge of a bridge. To my right, a plane passes overhead, moving in the direction from which I came. It looks so close! And yet, I reason, it must be farther away than it appears, otherwise it would be much larger. This reminds me I have always had a problem with perspective, with visualizing great distances and spaces.

I end up standing on one side of the stone bridge gazing out at the most magnificent view! The panorama stretches for as far as I can see, and the elevation is so great, the ground below isn't even visible. This is a dream, obviously, and yet the protective wall feels very real. What to do? There is really no question. I step onto the wall, intending to throw myself into the sky despite, or especially because, I fear there is a slight chance I might actually plummet downward. But of course I know I won't. As I perch on it, the wall bounces gently up and down beneath my feet, a little like an ocean buoy.

The vastness before me—interspersed with layers of cloud cover beyond which I perceive extremely distant mountains—is composed of soft, rich hues akin to dream watercolors, with blues and greens predominating. But there is nothing painting-like about the view, on the contrary. I can feel the absolute life and reality of the scene, and of its crowning glory—three oval bands of golden light resting on their sides, like concentric rings, which I don't so much see as experience in a vision.

Spreading my arms wide, I cry out exultantly, "My Lord! I love you with all my might!" and leap off the bridge.

The atmosphere completely supports me as I add quietly, "Which, I admit, has been pretty pathetic until lately" sensing God will appreciate my humble humor. In a standing position, I begin ascending at a phenomenal speed. I am not flying, I am being pulled upward. Years ago, in my first spontaneous lucid dreams, whenever I found myself caught in this mysterious gravitational pull, I was terrified of rocketing straight out into space, and not being able to return to earth. Not anymore; tonight I am ready to go wherever this force takes me.

I seem to stabilize at a certain level. The sky all around me is still indescribably vast, but filled now with a stormy power. The panorama is partially obscured by soft blue-green horizontal layers of clouds that roil gently, like an ocean of air intersected here and there by colossal black twisters. One of these massive black funnels is approaching me, but I resist the urge to try and change course to avoid it. The spinning vortex of darkness passes directly in front of me, seemingly close, yet I know it must be farther away than it appears, for I'm as small as a speck of dust in this heavenly storm.

The twister hovers close by, and I feel gravity pulling me toward it. I do not resist; I allow myself to be drawn toward this black tunnel, thinking that perhaps it will lead me somewhere. I struggle not to be afraid of uniting with a force so much greater than my physical body, because in a dream, I am the indestructible awareness of my soul. Still, it is not an appealing prospect, and I don't mind at all when the invisible current I'm floating in shifts me away from the black vortex. As I spin around slowly, I can still see the twister hovering ominously nearby, almost as though it sees me as well, and wants me. And as I gaze at it, the living darkness condenses into the shape of a massively built man... a pitch-black demon leaping across the sky toward me!

I cry, "My Lord, save me!" and the demon abruptly shrinks into an almost silly-looking cartoon that runs away from me in the direction from which the twister originally came. I say, "Of course You will" meaning there was never any doubt God would protect me.

Slowly, gently, I slip into void space. The darkness here is a soft, luminous gray, as if from all the starry universes latent within it, like floating in a Divine womb. Then far away, yet close by and almost directly ahead of me, a vision wrests the cry from me, "My Lord!" as a great golden flowing light, a liquid solid that is *everything*, rises out of the darkness on some random horizon, just one of endless possible horizons. But it is more accurate to say that Its rising *is* the horizon, *creates* the horizon. The bottom of a golden solar disc spills its breathtakingly beautiful Living Light so that a dimensional line, with a slight downward curve, forms below it—a Shen ring, the ancient Egyptian symbol for eternity! The beauty of it! My joy! The absolute splendor of God! Slowly, I wake.

Later that night, I dream I'm walking through a white stone courtyard surrounded on at least two sides by residential apartments. The living conditions are decent but poor. An Indian woman and her little girl walk out of one of the buildings.

Following them toward another entrance, I realize I'm dreaming.

I cross the threshold into a foyer that feels like the one in the beginning of my earlier lucid dream, but doesn't look remotely like it. An Indian man wearing blue-green medical scrubs strides past me, brushing up against me as he does so. It occurs to me then that this building is a hospital or clinic, and might be a good place to get a lucid check up to make sure all is well with my physical health.

I hurry up to the doctor, who has stopped to talk on a phone set in the wall, and grabbing his arm, tell him, "I want you to help me." He ignores me and, hanging up, begins walking away. What I do next, I don't consciously intend, and it happens so fast, I don't have time to think about my selfish and unethical behavior. But just for an instant, I'm surprised, because I've never behaved like this in a lucid dream before. Quickly, I cast a spell of irresistible beauty over myself and, gripping his arm again, easily get his attention this time. Smiling, I command, "Come with me" and he follows me obediently out of the building.

A pale-skinned young man with reddish-gold hair, who I assume is the doctor's assistant, follows us. We all sit down cross-legged in the courtyard next to a wall, the two men facing me. I inform the doctor that I want him to give me an overall health assessment, a lucid check up. He and the younger man both appear delighted by the prospect, but only because, I realize, it means I will be obliged to remove my clothes. So I dispel the desire part of my spell, leaving only their willingness to help me, and point at the small mole on my chest as I ask, "Is it melanoma?"

The older man, now smiling sedately, like my own personal zombie doctor, considers for a moment before answering, "Yes."

This is distressing! "But it's not deep, right?" I say, as though I can make it so.

He then goes on to tell me, at length, about a mutant strain of skin cancer, and how some people are not able to handle it, or how their bodies store it and can't get rid of it. I do *not* like what I am hearing. It sounds really bad. Then he commands me to take off all my clothes so he can operate on me, remove the diseased mole, right there and then.

I consider this idea; perhaps I can heal myself in this lucid dream through the symbolic action of removing the problem. I lift my shirt, but do not take off all my clothes; I see no reason to make myself completely vulnerable to them.

Leaning very close to me, his mouth beside my left ear, the doctor, who I can only describe as a demonic Depak Chopra, begins removing my mole. I feel the distinct sensation of him digging into my skin, ostensibly with a scalpel, but I experience no pain.

The procedure goes on for some time, during which I am helpless to do anything but marvel at the realistic sensation of his probing, even as I grow increasingly troubled. Something doesn't feel right about this, and it only gets worse when he begins speaking quietly into my ear, describing, in astonishing detail, the dangers of Purgatory, especially the areas closest to hell. Then he sits back, finished with his procedure.

As the young man smiles at me in an odd, knowing way, I thank them for their help.

False Awakening: I get out of bed, and head for the public bathroom around the corner to my right. It's dark inside. Finding the light switch, I flip it up, and am a little surprised, but very glad, when the lights flicker on. I enter a stall, where I find my dream notebook; I must have left it there the last time I got up to record my first dream of the night. But as I flip through it, I discover all the pages are either written on, or have been chewed away as though by mice. There is not a single clean piece of paper big enough to write on. Okay, I get it, this must be a false awakening.

Exiting the bathroom, I walk around a stone-lined garden bed, planted with grass and other green plants, wondering if what that doctor did to me in my last lucid dream actually worked. I reach up and touch my chest. Not feeling the mole there anymore, I think—It would be a miracle if my mole was gone when I woke up. But again, something doesn't feel right, the prospect does not make me happy, instead it worries me. I know it's possible I was healed, because everything is possible with God, the problem is, I don't feel God had anything to do with that second lucid dream. Then I'm arrested by a terrible sight: In a small dry fountain, a plump little bird is lying in a dark-red pool of its own blood, writhing weakly, yet with a vigorous desire to live. It is painfully obvious to me that something, or someone, tried to kill it. The sight distresses me deeply. This is not good, it is not good at all. The bird is a symbol of the soul, perhaps of my soul. I wake for real.

In my final dream of the night, I'm standing on our mountain top on a soft, clear morning, my long hair dyed black again. I am despondent, disturbed by my last lucid dream. As though He has always been there, a Man steps up behind me, and His presence feels like the dream space itself embracing me when gently but firmly, He says, "Don't be silly. Read your leaders."

I wake feeling blessed, deeply humbled, and profoundly encouraged.

My thought processes from the dream continue all day:
Did I actually injure myself in the reverse of a lucid dream healing, and transform a benign mole into a melanoma? I feel I have betrayed my own soul through this last lucid dream, in which I behaved as I never have before, casting spells to control people! And enlisting the assistance of a medical doctor, thereby turning the dream space into a hospital. What a nightmare! Bad, yet somehow not surprising, like the inevitable shadow cast by my first glorious lucid dream of the night.

Still, I was much too easy prey for the devil's temptations. If I'm worried about a little mole, I should simply go to the dermatologist. The dream space is sacred, and its healing powers should be requested through prayer only when truly necessary.

And who was the red-haired, pale-skinned young man who accompanied me outside with the demonic doctor? I remember now that he told me his name was "Matt", which just happens to be the name of a character from the fantasy series I recently finished, *The Wheel of Time* by Robert Jordan. Matt is very funny, the jester of the bunch, yet he is also a general in the Army of the Light fighting the forces of evil. I wonder if an angel was sent to watch over me during my encounter with the demonic doctor, who lasciviously whispered into my ear all those gruesomely detailed descriptions of the section of Purgatory adjacent to hell. The memory of Matt's understanding smile seems to encourage me not to be too worried about this dream, but instead to laugh at myself, albeit sadly, and with great humility.

I can guess now where the twister demon from my first lucid dream of the night was running—into my second lucid dream, where it got to me through my own weaknesses. But, I feel, only because God permitted it to do so, while at the same time sending along a smiling angel to watch over me during the ordeal, which I inflicted upon myself by being too afraid to deal with what I was afraid of.

And yet... does the bloodied bird perhaps indicate that I might have done some physical damage to myself through this dream, and transformed a harmless mole into melanoma through the dark power of fear? The mole looks and feels exactly the same this morning. Fearing it might be melanoma is what kept me away from the dermatologist in the first place. The devil relishes our fear, and leverages it whenever, and in any way, possible. I thought in the dream that I had chosen to cast a spell of irresistible beauty over myself to secure the doctor's services. I have never done such a thing before in a lucid dream, and have never done it since. It seems to me now that it was the devilish doctor who actually put me under *his* spell when he brushed up against me before pretending to ignore me.

I saw the bird of my soul, dying and powerless to save itself, in a dried up fountain filled only with its own blood. I feel this vision was delivered by my Spirit as a warning, but also as a promise of my soul's salvation through the power of Christ's blood. Unless, by arrogantly believing I can live and fly all on my own self-centered power, I deliberately cut myself off from the Life Giving Water of God's Love.

I know and feel in my soul it was Christ who stepped up beside me on our mountain top, the brief yet supremely sweet dream that is the crowning glory of last night's lucid marathon. His kind but firm voice urging, "Don't be silly" did much to wash away the bad taste left in my soul by the second dream with its false awakening, and to help me focus on the infinite hope revealed to me in the first dream. "Read your leaders" is a message I can clearly understand, for I have already begun downloading onto my Kindle books by prominent Christian writers, beginning with Saint Theresa of Avila.

For the first time in the little more than three years since I have been lucid dreaming on a regular basis, I feel I am beginning to truly understand my experiences.

◐

After these dreams, I made an appointment with a

dermatologist, which turned out to be a delightful experience. The woman was Italian, and full of life and good cheer. She took one look at my "mole" and waved it away with a, "That's nothing, just an age mark." Quickly examining me all over, she concluded cheerfully, "You have beautiful skin! Beautiful! Get out of here!"

Not only was my scary mole not melanoma, it can never even *be* melanoma.

> Worry, to Padre Pio, indicated a lack of faith. Since prayer was capable of opening the heart of God, what reason was there to be anxious? Faith in Jesus should shield the believer from all fear. A person with troubles should understand that they are tests sent from the Lord, intended to bring the person to a higher level of sanctity. For that reason, calm acceptance is a better response than useless worry. In the end, the person's soul will benefit from the test.[65]

God's Protection

Dream of May 30, 2014

I become aware of swinging high above the ground perched on a wooden tree swing. Far below me to my right, I glimpse Mami sitting on a park bench. Without any effort on my part, the swing moves like a great pendulum, forward and backward, taking me higher and higher, so that on one pass I'm leaning forward at a dramatic angle, and on the next pass I'm lying on my back in the sky. It makes me nervous how far above the earth

I am, as does the fact that I can't control the momentum of my swings.

My uneasiness intensifies even as I struggle to fight it, and this inner conflict generates a spark of lucidity... Yes, I'm dreaming, and I can fly, which means I won't fall. I hesitate a moment, then let go. I suffer a stab of fear as I plummet toward the ground, but at the last moment, I take control by intending to land on my feet as lightly as a feather, which I manage to do, but I lose lucidity and slip into other dreams...

I become aware of walking through our house at night. The central corridor is much longer than in waking reality, and the whole place feels slightly different, as though it's located somewhere else. But when I see Stinger enter the bedroom, I know for sure we live here. I pause to study the two separate beds, with mine, on the right, much larger than his bed, which is flush with the wall and narrower. He is already asleep under the covers.

I look around me, distracted from wondering why there are two beds instead of one by the fact that the room is missing two walls, and opens onto a steep snow-covered slope rising onto flat ground. It is daylight outside, so I am able to clearly make out the horizontal profiles of two obviously dead men, their bodies buried beneath the snow with only their features exposed. Their pale faces are handsome in a cold, profoundly disturbing way.

I lay down on my bed and stare at the two chilling profiles, unable to understand what they are doing there. Then the expression on one of the faces changes slightly... it seems to be coming back to life... My unease intensifies, and becomes full-blown panic when both bodies rise up out of their snowy graves and, grinning with evil intent, quickly make their way down the hill into our completely exposed bedroom. My cries of alarm have woken Stinger, but we are completely helpless as the undead men climb into bed with us, obviously intent on killing us, and maybe even devouring us!

Crossing my two index fingers, I raise them before me and cry, "Stop! In the name of God!" I repeat this command over and over as Stinger follows my example, making the sign of the cross with both hands. I then cross both my index fingers over both my thumbs, making two crosses, one for each demon. They can't seem to come any closer to us, but they aren't going away either.

At this point, something happens which is nearly impossible to describe. Closing my eyes, I open my mouth, and a Force emanates from inside it with a sound that is quiet in the sense that when a noise is too loud, too explosive, it deafens the ear drums, registering as more of a muffled vibration. Behind my eyelids, I perceive what looks like an elongated portal into greenish-black depths which are not liquid, not solid, not starry, yet might be all of these things even while it is also none of them. This vision lasts a mere instant, but when I open my eyes again, the undead demons have vanished as though vaporized, blinked out of existence. It was I who opened my mouth, but the Power that emerged from within me was not mine, of that I have no doubt. It was God who protected us, and saved us...

My next dream is one of those hyper real dreams that looks

and feels so much like being awake, I have no clue I'm dreaming... I'm sitting on one side of the Den (where my lucid dreaming bed would be) talking on the phone with Mami. As I gaze across the room at the four tall Bay Windows, I see a really large hawk, as big as a great Egyptian falcon, fly leisurely into view, and then begin coasting back and forth in front of the windows, drawing closer and closer to the house.

"Mami!" I whisper, "there is the most magnificent hawk just outside the window! It is *so* beautiful! Such brilliant colors! I've never seen a hawk this close up before!"

I continue describing the experience to her, telling her how special it is, how scarcely believable it is that the hawk is still here. It feels like a very special gift to be given this long, breathtaking view of such an awe inspiring bird, which appears to be deliberately paying me a visit.

Gradually, I notice that the great bird's somewhat velvety, charcoal-gray body is unusually long... as long as a man's... a man whose outstretched arms are the great wings. Ending the phone call, I walk tentatively over to the Bay Windows, feeling the beautiful creature wants me to come closer.

I'm only a few steps from the glass panes when my heart almost seems to stop as the man-size bird flies right up to the window on my far left and, hovering there, stares directly at me. It is waiting! I experience a slight thrill of fear, of sublime trepidation, but I know I'm protected by the glass, and that it can't, that it *won't*, hurt me. My hesitation only lasts a heartbeat before I step up to the window, sink down onto one knee, and rest my forehead against Its forehead.

Up close, my vision is filled by deep black, large and soft, oval eyes. What I feel as I gaze directly into these mysterious portals is impossible to put into words. I sense we are now joined in some inscrutable, transcendent, undeniable way.

Standing again, I take about three steps back, my hands clasped before me, and the experience climaxes when the falcon nods at me, inclining its head in utterly human-like acknowledgment of what has passed between us. I feel I should say something, perhaps "Namaste" but that word feels flimsy, inadequate. There is nothing I can possibly say, all I can do is stand there with my hands clasped in a silent prayer of reverent gratitude...

My brother has joined me in the Den, and I am joyfully trying to describe to him my experience with the divine falcon. "Nothing like this has ever happened before!" I exclaim, and in response to one of his quiet questions, I assure him that, "No, I didn't have anything to do with it!" meaning it wasn't my imagination, my wishful interpretation of the event, or any of those things, it really, truly happened...

I'm reclining across a bed, which is even more exposed than the bed from my earlier dream because it is placed out on the portico of a white temple. Everything is a pure white. The moment I become conscious of where I am, two lovely female demons with long, sharp nails pounce onto the bed with me. Like vampires thirsting for my blood, they lean over me, going hungrily for my throat. But they cannot touch me. They cannot get to me. I see the frustration on their faces as I sense, close behind me in the temple, two men ready to help me if I need them. In my mind's eye, I glimpse their golden hair and short white flowing garments. But I don't seem to need their help, because all I have to do is think of God protecting me, and the demons are banished. I know this is a blessing of the falcon I communed with earlier.

> But the Lord is faithful, he will strengthen you and guard you from the evil one.[66]

> Be aware of this: The demons were not created as the figures we now call 'demons,' because God made nothing evil. They were created good, but having fallen from heavenly wisdom, they now grovel on earth... jealous... they constantly set up roadblocks on the path to heaven because they don't want us ascending to where they have fallen from.[67]

I shared the dream of the falcon with my mother, who commented that the Holy Spirit came to me in a way familiar to my soul by evoking my novel of Hatshepsut, who by being crowned Pharaoh became the Female Falcon.

> The falcon shares much of the solar symbolism of the eagle, with which it can change places. It is aspiration, victory, ascension through all planes... Thought to be able to fly up to the sun and gaze unwaveringly upon it

and to identify with it, it is Christ gazing on the glory of God; carrying its young to the sun, it is Christ bearing souls to God; plunging to take fish out of the sea, it is Christ rescuing souls from the sea of sin. Thought to renew its plumage by flying up to the sun and plunging into the sea, it symbolizes resurrection and the new life in baptism; the soul renewed by grace. It also represents the inspiration of the Gospels, hence its use as a lectern. Grasping the serpent in its talons, it is victory over sin.[68]

But those who trust in the Lord will find new strength. They will soar high on wings like eagles... Isaiah 40:31[69]

John the Evangelist, the author of the fourth gospel account, is symbolized by an eagle.[70]

Soon after this dream, my mother sent me the film *The Gospel of John* which I treasure, feeling as did Saint Theresa:

If they loved Him they would delight in looking at pictures of Him, just as they take pleasure in seeing pictures of anyone else whom they love.[71]

Beloved

Dream of June 13, 2014

I have a very vivid experience of walking around the house to my black car. I'm surprised when I slip on the driveway, which I realize then is covered with a fine sheet of almost invisible ice, obliging me to grab hold of the door handle, and carefully pull myself into the car. Turning the key in the ignition, I am abruptly plunged into darkness. Losing all visuals, I both hear and feel a powerful rumbling sound as I spin into nothingness with the final thought—Okay, I'm about to die in an earthquake, this is the end...

I wake up in that instant, surprised to still be alive. The experience was very disturbing. It seems I heard and felt the loud sounds and strong vibrations that sometimes characterize the beginning of an out of body experience, yet I was already embedded in a dream scene so true-to-life, that when I lost all visuals, I could only interpret the experience as some kind of natural disaster. I was already out of body, and was suddenly yanked back in. Weirdly powerful.

I go back to sleep, and suffer a false awakening in a bedroom that belongs to Stinger and me. I answer a phone call... Lost time...

Where I find myself is ostensibly still part of our bedroom, but it has no solid boundaries. The atmosphere is the deep gray of void space, and there is no bottom to it, no floor, no ceiling, no walls. A tall clothes dresser—set against what I vaguely feel is a back corner wall—is the only thing that provides a sense of three dimensional space. My Lover and I are sitting on this dresser, in each others arms. His face is less than a breath away from mine, and we are smiling at each other with an intimacy that transcends words. Our closeness is beyond my ability to understand. We are together, and that is all that is, and all that matters!

He is perfectly beautiful, His features, and His lean body, all clearly defined, His skin, like mine, a soft white, as though we are made of moonlight. He is my Lover, yet He is also my spouse. What I feel in our embrace is a perfect love indistinguishable from joy, and from the essence of who I am. What I feel being with Him is my very soul, our togetherness flowing like a dance as we constantly move in each others arms. I know this is not waking reality, but neither is it a dream, it is real, its own state of being, very special and rare. When we are together like this, nothing is held back, nothing is missing, I have everything I can possibly desire.

Occasionally, I plunge off the dresser, but His hands are always holding mine, and this slipping, then being pulled back up by Him and to Him, is wondrous, only seeming dangerous because, as I tell Him, "I trust you not to let me fall."

My Beloved begins removing my clothing, which is entirely white, and the experience is a stripping away of all barriers between us, a pure sensuality of the soul. My shirt rising up over my head, I plunge downward in front of the dresser, and for an instant, I feel in danger of falling into nothingness, but I'm aware the danger is not real for I know He will never let go of me.

Both of us sitting naked on top of the dresser, I look down at His body, and distinctly see his shining male sex, which looks carved of black obsidian and stands erect as a column partially merged with the temple-like wall of his belly. His phallus looks hard as stone, yet also glimmers like the black life-filled potency of deep space, and it is cradled in what looks like the hollowed out trunk of a tree, with three "straps" crossing over it near the top that appear to be containing its power.

Abruptly, I find myself back in normal space, in the dream bedroom where I thought I woke up earlier to answer the phone. Slipping off the dresser, my Lover, smiling at me, says, "I have to write another report now" as He stretches himself across my bed and begins typing on my laptop. The room is now lit by bright sunlight, and I am pleased to see the ocean extending just off the porch.

I wake for real. Some time later—after getting up to write my dream notes, and praying for a dream that will confirm my Lover and Spouse is truly who I feel He is—I fall asleep again...

I become aware of holding a little boy's hand, my brother's hand. He is pulling me eagerly along behind him, and I realize my entire family is following a very special Man who is leading us somewhere. As we turn a corner, I glimpse my late friend Sara standing behind us, and am very happy she can see us following this special Person. My brother is so intensely happy, he keeps tugging me along, urging me to run faster so we don't lose sight of our Guide, who I suddenly understand is the Man from my earlier dream, my Lover, and I know I'm right about who I feel He is.

We begin climbing a staircase, where I catch up with my maternal grandfather. He looks as he did in his early nineties, shortly before he died, but he is vigorous enough to take two steps at a time, and I fondly comment on this fact as I help him reach the landing. My brother has run ahead of me down a long dark corridor ending in a wooden door. He and I are alone up here for the moment, and as I walk toward the door, I become fully present in the dream, gently but deeply excited to be lucid.

My brother opens the door, and as he crosses the threshold, I pause to gaze out at him where he stands on the flat roof of the building looking just as he does now. He is not a child anymore but a grown man wearing an old-fashioned black bowler hat.

When I try to speak his name, I can't find my voice. I try again, and this time manage to say loudly and clearly, "Mario, esto es un sueño." ("This is a dream.")

Turning to look at me, he steps back inside, and stares directly into my eyes as though he understands.

I repeat, "Esto es un sueño."

He turns around again, and walks back out into the night.

I follow him across the large rooftop, where I catch up with him and say impatiently, "This is a dream, stupid!"

We are *very* high up. Below us stretches the blue-black water of an immense crescent-shaped ocean bay. The building on which we're standing seems to be a lighthouse a few miles from the shore, all along which rises a magnificent sky-blue city made entirely out of what looks like crystal, with golden lights shining everywhere within it. The view is incomparably beautiful.

"Mario, what do you see?" I ask. "Tell me what you see, so that in the morning we can remember it together." I desperately want him to be a witness to this heavenly city.

But he just stands there, and murmurs something that lets me know he probably isn't lucid anymore, if he ever was. As I gaze at his face, wondering how I can snap him into lucidity, I wake.

Almost my entire family was following our Lord up the stairs. Even my late best friend was there. Sara was Jewish, but after her death, when I was helping transcribe her boxes of writing, I was astonished to discover some of the last poems she wrote, just before she died, were about Christ.

I had prayed for another dream that would confirm the identity of the Man in my first dream, the dream of my Beloved. I asked, and I received.

A dresser is where we keep our clothing, which for me has always symbolized the flesh the soul is wearing, stripped off at the moment of death. My first transcendent dream of the night speaks for itself, so that it almost seems rude, a mental intrusion, to touch and deconstruct it with words. I knew what was happening was neither a dream or waking reality. The experience was a gift, what Saint Theresa of Avila refers to as a divine favor. I was purely my soul in the arms of the Lord.

> When His Majesty wills to bestow on us any supernatural favors, we experience the greatest peace, calm, and sweetness in the inmost depths of our being; I know neither where nor how... We can do nothing on our own part to gain this favor; it comes from God alone; therefore let us not strive to understand it.[72]

And these words by Julian of Norwich eloquently express how I continue to feel:

> God allows us to fall, but by the joy, strength, and wisdom of Divine love we are kept safe—and by mercy and grace, we are lifted up within the many facets of Divine joy. In this way, through both generous mercy and stringent straightness of heart, God wants us to endlessly see and love the Divine presence in our lives. When we look at life from this perspective, we are filled with contentment and eternal joy.[73]

I *will* comment on the final part of the dream, where my Lover's phallus was the central column in a temple that looked and felt like the universe embodied. Certainly the particular predilections of my soul, for so long enamored of ancient Egypt, had something to do with the "style" of this vision.

> Hatshepsut felt short of breath recalling what the high priest had said about these columns as their upward thrusting force excited her like never before. She was surrounded by the virile power of God manifesting in shafts of Divine procreative light that conceived the universe in a sperm-like shower of stars.[74]

The three "straps" crossing over this living column enclosing, containing, cradling God's unfathomable Power and Mystery, I feel represent the Holy Trinity.

If He is truly infinite and transcendent, the truth about God cannot be fully grasped by the finite mind... The work, and even more so, the very nature of God, cannot appear to the human mind as anything short of mystery. This mystery typically presents itself to us as a series of paradoxes. God is one, yet God is three. Jesus is human, yet Jesus is divine. These paradoxes are truths-intension; they strain the brain and summon the human mind to bow in awe and worship.[75]

Chapter Eleven – Purification

Faith knows no fear
this is what it means
to comport myself
like a lady of Heaven
graceful and attentive
to the Lord of Life

Maid of Honor

Dream of July 3, 2014

The moment I see Him, the dream comes into focus. But, as always happens, nothing except His presence, and receiving the blessing of His attention, matters. I have no thought for anything else, not even the realization that I'm dreaming. I am in His presence, and that in itself is a dream come true, whether I am awake or asleep. I am standing before Him, one of perhaps several people on a platform, or a stage of some kind. He is seated nearby facing us, or rather, we are facing Him. A woman who is very special is seated on His left.

I can't remember what is said, or why we are here, all I can do is wonder—Did He just meet my eyes? Is it my imagination, or is He looking over at me? Is He taking special notice of me? Does He see me?!

In these dreams, I am always conscious of being special to Him, but tonight I'm not so sure it isn't just wishful thinking on my part. And yet—as always when He is near—I am conscious of, I can feel, my inner beauty, the glow of my soul, and I know in my heart that He sees me.

I realize then that my mother is standing just a few feet away, and that He is listening to her describe, in her passionately detailed way, an experience she had recently, blessing her with His undivided attention.

I say, "Mami..." interrupting her. This makes her a bit angry, and I regret interfering simply because I was getting impatient, and a little jealous. But as a result, my Lord is looking at me now. Even though I wish I had gotten his attention in another, more deserving way, it is still bliss to feel His eyes on me.

There is much more to this dream... a small group of us spend a lot of time in His company, His regard never directly focused on me specifically... Then I'm walking in a darkness that feels like a passage from one space to another, when I suddenly brush up against my beloved Lord, who is now standing beside me.

I say eagerly, "I'm going to try and have a lucid dream with you tonight."

Looking down into my eyes, His smile subdued, He replies, "Is that so? But then you won't even share it."

Speaking clearly, I assure Him, "I have a lucid dreaming Blog. I tell it *all.*"

Abruptly, He asks me, "How would you like to be Maid of Honor at the Wedding?"

I am stunned. I know about this special event (it may have been the subject under discussion earlier) but I can't quite believe He has chosen me for this role. "I would love to!" I declare, basking in the intimacy between us.

His black suit blending with the darkness, the skin of His face indistinguishable from the flesh-colored illumination enabling me to see Him, He steps even closer to me and says quietly, "Backstage..."

I seem to have returned home, where I ecstatically declare to someone, "You know what this means? It means Papi is going to have to spend a fortune on a dress for me!" and see a vision of myself walking down the isle in a long golden dress.

Then, somehow, my Lord is still there, observing me with a subtle air of approval, as I strive to remember everything we talked about by writing it down on a piece of raw, blood-red meat into which I carve the words...

I continue excitedly telling everyone I come across that He asked me to be Maid of Honor at the Wedding, and to dine with Him! Yet the people I'm confiding my joy to are trying to sober me up. I don't remember what they say exactly, but they are essentially telling me I can never really be with Him, that my desire to be with Him, fully and forever, can never actually be satisfied. But to all their warnings, I reply passionately, with all my heart, "I would be happy with just one of His toe nails!" and in that moment, I experience prostrating myself face down on the ground before Him and joyfully, humbly, ecstatically kissing one of His big toes, truly feeling this is blessing enough for me!

Then my awareness rises completely out of my body, so that I am observing myself seated in a white void, and this detached part of me thinks—Now is when I begin to feel despair. The thought is accompanied by an extreme close-up view of my eyes filling with greenish lines that cross my irises like bars. Immediately, I banish them with a passionate—No! I will not feel despair, because I will never again surrender my Faith.

I become aware of Papi, who seems to have been around for some time, and then, very far away, I also see my maternal grandmother. I am "outside" now in a white "daylight" that has the feel of an ocean shore, and Abuelita is visible where she is making her way through a series of long narrow impressions in the white "sand". She is obliged to navigate across them, and is not having an easy time of it. I wish I could just run to her, and she to me, but that is not possible.

As Papi continues silently observing me, I cry out to my grandmother, excited to share my glorious news with her, "Abuela! He asked me to be Maid of Honor at the Wedding!"

She yells back, her voice faint with distance, "At His wedding!"

"Yes! And He asked me to dine with Him!"

As I feel her sharing in my joy as I wake.

That morning I wrote: This was a Deep Dream, between 2-2:30 a.m.

I tell him eagerly, "I'm going to try to have a lucid dream with you tonight..." Here I echo His words to me in that seminal dream *"I'm going to try to..."* and His response *"But then you won't even share it"* seems to refer to the doubt I've been having lately about the book I'm writing, *Lucid Dreams and the Holy Spirit*, doubts I dismiss by recalling what Saint Theresa of Avila says about doubts and the devil. But the uncertainties linger as I wonder if anyone but me will appreciate my dreams, and how He is revealing Himself to me through them. In this particular dream, He seems to be encouraging me to tell it all, and not to doubt this is what He wants me to do, for it is His will I share my dreams of Him. I should not be concerned by how the book will be received.

My soul is the Bride, my mind is the Maid of Honor, my thoughts the Bridesmaids, and my Bridegroom is Christ. It is my soul's union with God I am joyfully cultivating in my dreams, both awake and asleep. This little book is an invitation to others to attend my personal relationship with the Holy Spirit, and to share in its joy, as I toss it into the world like a bridal bouquet.

> Our pious forefathers believed in spiritual preparation, and they said so. They saw themselves as a bride being prepared to meet the bridegroom. They regarded this earth as the dressing room to outfit themselves for heaven.[76]

I distinctly remember my Lord saying quietly to me, "Backstage" where dressing rooms are traditionally located.

When I told him, *"I'm going to try and have a lucid dream with you tonight"* I think I was expressing what I feel and believe—that the ability to lucid dream, and to dream share, is a valid way of experiencing and glorifying God, a way of revealing, exploring and deepening the truth of the interconnectedness of consciousness—a modern way of expressing the fact that every soul has its life in God, for we are the children of His heart, and all of Creation is how He expresses His love.

Day by Day

Dream of July 17, 2014

My Lord, the Holy Spirit, speaks to me, He is very near, right beside me, I see Him clearly as He earnestly tells me, "You are very special to me... You are close to me... and you *will* be."

I partially wake, joyfully recalling His words to me, elated by the promise "and you *will* be." I continue repeating what I heard Him say as I wake up completely, and realize I just saw Him, was with Him!

"And you *will* be."

I can scarcely grasp the sweet immensity of this promise, spoken in a warm, almost urgent tone brimming with love and approval. The dream was fleeting, but I remember it vividly, and I still feel it imbuing me with a subtle but irrepressible strength indistinguishable from gratitude and happiness. I *am* close to him, yet I can grow ever closer to Him, know Him, and love Him, more deeply and dearly?! What a sweet, sweet promise! Like the lyrics of the song I sang and played the tambourine to in a third grade school production, a song I still love:

> Day by day, day by day,
> Oh, dear Lord, three things I pray
> To see thee more clearly

love thee more dearly
follow thee more nearly, day by day[77]

Taking Out the Trash

Dream of July 24, 2014

Some time after 4:00 in the morning, a light shines into my dreaming mind when, through the side window of a house I'm standing in, I see my Lord bending over to pick up my trashcan, then returning the somewhat dented, dark container to its place against a wall after having apparently emptied it for me. The lighting is clear, and everything is sharply visible to me because He is here. I am amazed He lowered Himself to perform this menial task for me. At the same time, it makes sense that He is helping me dispose of all my garbage.

As He disappears from view, walking toward the front of the house, I quickly leave the kitchen to follow Him. Through the living room window, I can see Him in the front yard (*the spacious suburban lawn in no way resembles my waking reality mountain home*.) He is interacting with my husband, and a third person. They appear to be relaxing together, playing some kind of game with a ball. I don't actually see a ball, it's more like I feel something being shared between them. My Lord is relaxing with my husband out in our front yard! I simply have to capture this on film!

I quickly fetch my camera, knowing He won't stay for long, but even as I run outside, I'm afraid it's already too late, for I see only my husband. Then, turning slightly, I spot my Lord several yards away leaning against the wall of a neighboring house. Wearing sand-colored slacks, and a white dress shirt with the sleeves partially rolled up, he looks both perfectly relaxed and alert. I finally have Him in my viewfinder, and the moment He sees me pointing the camera at him, He walks back toward our driveway. He is now in the frame with my husband, and I am ecstatic! Everyone will know He was here, that He paid us the unexpected, incredible honor of coming to visit us in the midst of the important work He is always doing.

But it's already time for Him to leave. Without speaking to me, or even glancing at me, He begins walking away. As my husband trails after Him, I know he works near Him, although not directly with Him. The third person, a woman who appears to be one of His close assistants, follows me to the front door as I walk back into the house. Standing on the threshold looking in, she urges me to accompany them to, "The Hall." I'm not sure that's what she called it, but I understand it is a very large, important place where all the world's affairs are administered.

Glancing down at my old shorts and orange t-shirt, I laugh and protest that I couldn't possibly go dressed like this. "Next time," I say, "let me know you're coming, and I'll be ready!"

Smiling broadly, she turns and follows Him.

Overjoyed, positively ecstatic, my little dog running eagerly in the wake of my joy, I begin skipping down the long central corridor of our house. Leaping forward, I almost manage to do the splits in mid-air like a ballerina, conscious now of wearing black yoga pants. I know I can't really dance like this... but yes, I can, because I'm so happy!

"Look at our beautiful home, Arthur! We live in such a beautiful place!"

Indeed, this spacious central corridor is lined with rooms, and there is a whole other second floor which is equally vast, and even more splendid. I can scarcely believe my husband and I live in such a beautiful Mansion, and yet I distinctly remember sitting in a blue-and-white room where I read for most of the day. I wonder why I need so much living space, but it makes sense that this glorious home, which feels literally endless, is where we live. Before I wake, I see a vision of an atmospherically lit room upstairs where all the furnishings are burnished to a soft golden hue.

> The filling with the Spirit, then, requires that we give up our all... that we rid our hearts of that centuries-old accumulation of Adamic trash and open all rooms to the heavenly Guest.[78]

I feel my Lord was showing me that my love and devotion to Him is not in conflict with my marriage. Framing them together with my dream camera seems to imply that I can help bring my husband closer to God, and help nurture his spiritual growth just as he has helped me with mine simply by loving and caring for me. My Lord wants me to trash, once and for all, any condescending views of my husband's spiritual depths I might be harboring, a fact He made clear by not even glancing at me once in this dream, a gentle reprimand.

> So let's stick with our spiritual practices and not grow careless. For the Lord, who works for good with everyone who chooses the good, gives us a helping hand.[79]

I was still wearing old house clothes, old habits of thinking and feeling. I should *always* be prepared to receive Him, to follow Him with every thought, but I cannot do so if I continue slipping into negative, selfish, prideful ways of thinking. I am blessed by my earthly spouse and circumstances, and to perceive them as distractions on the path of my spiritual growth will only hinder it.

> To the extent that they live together in love, man and woman become a picture of the inner life of God. This might be the most amazing thing that we can say about marriage.[80]

Like my husband, a federal employee, I too work for the government: for Christ's Kingdom—established and growing on Earth so that it may one day be like heaven. God has made it clear that is His plan, and it is our sacred duty to help make it happen. Because of Christ, human beings are once again the stewards of Creation, and God's intent will not be fulfilled until the world is once again as it was in the beginning, with mankind living "on earth as in heaven."

Dancing With the Prince

Dream of August 27, 2014

I'm driving Stinger and myself to a special service at St. Leo's church, the church of my childhood, attached to the school I attended for two years in Junior High. I turn right into the parking lot, and am astonished by the crowds of cars and people. I'm obliged to crawl along in order to avoid hitting children, seniors in wheelchairs, entire families. Everyone looks extremely happy, and oblivious to the risk of getting run over. I manage to navigate this obstacle course without any accidents, but now I'm worried there won't be any room left in the church, that we've come too late. So when I surprisingly come upon several empty parking spots, I quickly pull into one.

But now I have another problem. As I tell Stinger, "I forgot to include Arthur in the equation." I can't leave my dog in the car for so long, but I can't bring him into the service with me either, where he will undoubtedly squirm restlessly. I don't even think dogs are allowed in churches. St. Leo's feels much larger, much grander than it actually is, and I *really* want to go inside, but I can't figure out how to make that happen under the circumstances. Then I realize the procession toward the altar has begun, and everyone is part of it. All the parishioners—dressed now in elegant, quietly splendid Renaissance-style clothing of a satiny silver—are moving from the entrance to the church grounds toward the church itself. Oh, wow! It seems we can experience the service even while remaining outside...

No longer sitting in the car, I'm reclining, alone, on one of the countless divans arranged in semi-circular groups outside on the grass. The long dress I'm wearing is several shades of yellow-gold, and has flowing, veil-like sleeves.

The service has begun, and all my appreciative attention is focused on the woman who is the star. Tall and beautiful in a radiant white-gold gown, she is singing, her voice a clear, energetic, perfectly lovely soprano as she moves along the rows of parishioners. She too is a parishioner, and I find myself thinking she must get all the starring rolls in these church productions, for she must certainly be the prettiest, most talented woman in the congregation. I wonder if this makes her conceited, and if she is a disappointingly superficial Christian, primarily attached to the social aspect of the church, not truly in touch with the Holy Spirit.

I entertain these jealous speculations for a mere instant, because there can be no doubt she is genuinely marvelous; her voice seems to uplift the music itself. Everyone has eyes only for this very special handmaiden of God walking along the front row of parishioners as though singing to each person in turn. Then the Prince appears, His cloud-blue attire worthy of a Renaissance King, and when the Queen greets Him, He requests that she introduce Him to a lady worthy of becoming His future bride. Without hesitation, she turns in my direction, and walking around my divan, bends down to take my hand.

Intensely excited and honored, I rise from my seat, fully

intending to play my part as gracefully as possible. The Queen chose *me*! But I can't think about that now; what's important is fulfilling my role in in this sacred pageant, which means obeying its mysterious choreography. I must intuit the steps, feel them out, and execute them in perfect time with the Prince.

My shyness is not an act as I approach Him, and manage to execute a deep, slightly awkward curtsy in His honor. This is the first time in my life I have actually curtsied, and it feels odd, yet also wonderful, to express reverence with my whole body. All the while following the Prince's lead, I step into the dance. He turns in place, and I turn in place, my arms arching gracefully above my head as my skirts and veils billow gently around me.

When we are facing each other again, He raises his right arm, gently bent at the elbow in front of His chest, as if he is embracing someone, and I reflect the gesture. Inwardly, I panic for a second, worried I didn't raise the correct arm, but outwardly I don't break the flow of the dance, and we repeat the gesture with our left arms before once again turning in place.

I am awkwardly conscious of wearing my Italian leather house slippers beneath my golden dress, down the back of which I can feel my long, straight hair falling. I am acting, yet I am also truly feeling the gracefully reserved excitement of a lady chosen to dance with the Prince. After a final twirl, I cover up a slight stumble by taking a few steps back, my hands clasped over my womb as I bow my head, acknowledging the honor I have been awarded.

Deeply thrilled, I resume my seat feeling I did my part well enough, even though I *could* have done better. Why did the Queen choose me? What made me stand out? Does it really matter? I was only a minor part of the Pageant; I will soon be forgotten. But when I look back and see black-and-silver cameras, I realize the event is being filmed, and hope I can at least watch my performance afterward. I feel restless now, wishing I had done better, that I could play a larger part, that I could dance again.

I wake up feeling just as I did in the dream, restless, almost wanting to cry, filled with longing, dissatisfied, conflicted about my soul's desire to shine vs. ego vanity, the attachment to self we must surrender. Yet I long to dance, to be His bride at the Wedding, and to know my personal expression of grace will not be lost, but is forever captured on some Divine record. I desire more than anything to experience my true beauty—a spiritual attractive power of which the external fleeting good looks of physical youth is a mere shadow. I also realize I suffered those critical, jealous thoughts of the magnificent singer because *I* am the one who behaves as I was afraid she did; *I* am always the one who wants to be the star of whatever I'm involved in.

The film of the Pageant, in which I played only a fleeting part, reflects how I feel about my life, about how little I have yet actually contributed to the glory of God. It was only by the grace of the Queen that I was brought to the attention of the Prince of Peace.

This dream brought back memories of dancing in a college production of *Romeo & Juliet.* I recalled the thrill of being swept up by my partner, who twirled me around and around. I can be content with merely playing my own small part if I can dance, dance, dance forevermore with my Prince! When I woke up, I felt the sacred Pageant had barely begun, and that it would never really end.

The Queen of Heaven chose my soul as being worthy of becoming her Son's betrothed. Like every soul who hears the Word of God, I have a chance to be His bride at the Wedding to which my Lord invited me a few weeks ago in another dream. It is no longer about my ego wanting to be the star of the show, it is about my soul burning with love as I desire to dance forever with God.

Chapter Twelve – Discernment

Looking back on my life now
the more I know God always was
there even when I was not aware
my soul a child lost in this world
of ugly crowds violently arguing
I'm only imagining a loving Father
because we're really simply orphans
of thoughtless chemical reactions –
struggling until we die and vanish –
that I'm dreaming the kind Presence
I know in my thoughts and feelings
is treating me with synchronicities
keeping my little self fed and warm

Appearances

Dream of September 6, 2014

In the midst of dreams, I come upon a scene that captures my full attention. It's night time, and my Guardian Lord is standing at the top of a narrow flight of steps leading up out of an alley. He is supervising the secret process of sending individuals, whom He has personally chosen, up over the wall and out into the world, where they will strive to secure peace in the name of God. Lucidly entering this scene, I perch on the railing to my right, and glide slowly up the banister toward Him.

Continuing to usher the members of His team, one at a time,

over the wall and into the night, He looks down into my eyes as I consciously rise up toward him. Boldly, I pucker my lips to kiss Him, and He lowers His head as if to kiss me back, but although our mouths come very close, they do not touch.

I say petulantly, "You didn't kiss me" as I wonder why.

A hint of a teasing smile on His lips, He replies, "I thought I had competition tonight" and returns His attention to the individuals who continue emerging from the building. Leaping over the wall, they run courageously into what I know are dark and dangerous city streets all over the world.

Standing one or two steps beneath Him looking up, I'm able to get a close-up view of his face. For a moment, I study the pores in his skin, which looks completely, vulnerably human, before I wake.

That morning I wrote: Yesterday, I watched the final disc of HBO's *The Bible*. Despite my dislike of the actor who plays Jesus, and of the production in general, I was enthralled, for I have never before seen dramatized what happens after Christ's resurrection—the coming down of the Holy Spirit at Pentecost, followed by some of the Acts of the Apostles. I wept, and went to bed filled with a powerful love and longing for Christ.

Before falling asleep, I remembered again what Saint Theresa said about Christ, "If they loved Him they would delight in looking at pictures of Him, just as they take pleasure in seeing pictures of anyone else whom they love." I also thought about how much more I liked the actors who played Christ in the marvelous films *The Gospel of John* and *Jesus of Nazareth*. I pondered how it doesn't matter who plays Jesus as long as they are physically presentable and their performance truly inspired, for it is Christ, and his Word spoken by actors, that affects me so. Then it struck me how in my dreams, I have seen the traditional figure of Christ only a handful of times.

I do believe my Lord teased me last night! He has a sense of humor, of course! When he said, "I thought I had competition tonight" He seems to have been referring to the three other images of Jesus, played by three different actors, I had been thinking about in bed. It seems significant that last night He gave me the opportunity to look more closely at the face He has worn for me in most of my dreams. He let me see how those specific features are completely alive, yet, as I stared at His face, it also began to look like a mask to me. God is no more contained by the appearance He has taken in my dream space, than Christ is confined to the actors who play Him.

Last night is the closest I have come to being fully lucid in His Presence. I was intensely drawn to Him, but I did not feel overwhelmed, and scarcely able to think, perhaps because the form he assumed last night was so different from the traditional appearance of Jesus that had filled my heart and my thoughts just before I went to sleep.

Last night I also saw expressed, in the agents my Lord was ushering out into the cities of the earth, what I already understood mentally—the Holy Spirit works through all those who truly love and seek to help others in the name of God.

Through souls actively faithful to Christ and His teachings, God strengthens, expands and perfects His kingdom on earth. In my dream, I feel I witnessed the Holy Spirit, poised at the top of steps leading up out of the dark alley of our fallen nature, sending souls out into the world to do God's loving will.

My Lord has a sense of humor! I can't get over how He seems to have teased me by pretending to be jealous of the other images of Jesus I took to bed with me last night. He knew I had the traditional figure of Christ in my mind and heart, but still He showed Himself to me in the form in which I have come to know and adore Him.

The Comforter

Dream of September 30, 2014

Another night of vivid in depth "crazy" dreams in which I sometimes slip in and out of identities. When I woke, I felt my dreams were manifesting the fact that, by overturning the heavy stone of my ego and fully exposing it to the Light of the Son, aspects of my self—abruptly deprived of the dark obscurity in which they continued feeding on each other—are squirming in fear of being crushed, once and for all.

In my final dream of the night, I was working on my computer, just as I am now. It was daylight, and I think my brother was standing behind my right shoulder, when a Presence physically resembling Stephen Colbert wearing an exquisitely tailored black suit walked into the room. I knew in the dream that He visited me regularly, and it was wonderful to experience His company, but as I glanced back and saw He wasn't looking at me, I suffered a sinking despair. I thought—He doesn't really love me as I love Him, of course not. Why should He? He doesn't really notice me, He's only here because it's His responsibility. It's not really about me.

Listlessly, I kept working as He walked around my chair, coming close enough for me to lean my head against Him. I forgot all my doubts then as for a few moments, I felt deeply comforted, appreciated, and loved.

That morning I wrote: As soon as I dared to lean and rest against Him, I felt His Love and support. Brief as the contact was, this feeling has remained with me, and continues energizing me. A mere instant of feeling His closeness makes me happier than anything!

Interesting that last night He chose to come to me looking like Stephen Colbert, my brother in Christ. All of us who love and believe in God—in the Father, the Son and the Holy Spirit—are brothers and sisters, and the creative work we do in His name serves to enlighten, entertain and comfort us. Working together to help make it happen, we dream of the future when all will be on earth as in heaven.

> Our Divine Lover longs for us to cling to God with all our strength, so that we may identify ourselves with goodness and unity forever... God does not hold back

from a single aspect of Creation, nor does the Divine One disdain to serve us in the simplest and most ordinary ways... The Divine One is the essence of rest and security, the only true comfort. God wants to be known; the Divine One is pleased when we rest in the Spirit's presence, since all that was created will never be enough in and of itself to give us what we need.[81]

Update to my Dream Journal later that same day: I received even more comfort today. As I was driving home from the gym, I saw a huge, soft white cloud resting on our mountain top. But it wasn't raining, and the rest of the world below was hot and sunny. Then, as I turned onto the little lane leading up to our mountain road, a flash of white amidst the trees prompted me to think—I should be open to a communication from the Holy Spirit today.

An instant later, I hit the brake and gasped out loud when an immense bald eagle flew directly in front, and just slightly above, my windshield. The awesome bird passed leisurely in front of my car, then turned around and flew directly before my windshield again, before swooping back to grace me with a third view of its majesty before vanishing into the woods. Instead of the great falcon I communed with in a recent dream, I saw a bald eagle. We have been living on the mountain almost five years now, and I have never seen an eagle here before.

Because we are within God, everything will always be about God, if I truly look and listen.

Where Did Abuela Go?1

Dream of October 3, 2014 *Today would have been Abuela's Birthday. She was 77 when she died twenty years ago.*

My sister and I are at work in a great department store, but we are getting ready to leave sooner than later. I'm aware of Abuela (*our maternal grandmother*) waiting for us at the front of the store. She is dressed all in black, but elegantly, not because she is in mourning. Lourdes and I are busy going about our business, standing close together near the front of the store. But, apparently, we are taking longer than expected, because I suddenly realize Abuela is no longer there.

I say, "Where did Abuela go?"

My sister shares my concern, and we quickly leave the store to look for her. We reason she must have decided to wait for us beside the car, which is only a couple of blocks away, but the streets are so crowded with people and traffic, it's impossible to see that far. My concern grows by the second, because this is not like her; she always waits for us.

We reach the car, but Abuela isn't there. Anxiously, we enter the building beside it, hoping she decided to pass some time in there while waiting for us. It's dark inside the pub-restaurant, and as we walk down the whole long length of it, my concern escalates to a full blown panic. In a small room just off the back exit, I tell my sister, "Try calling her!" Of course! Why didn't we try calling her phone before? Lourdes makes the call, but ends up talking to someone else, and urging them to find our brother.

Hurrying outside, I exclaim impatiently, "We know where our

brother is!" But Abuela is still missing. She has completely disappeared! Where could she possibly have gone? Why did she leave us?

There's nothing we can do except return to the great department store where we last saw her, with the faint hope she also went back there looking for us.

We walk into the expansive building through the back entrance, and there He stands, in a white dress shirt rolled up to his elbows over sand-colored slacks. He is talking with another man, some kind of manager. I am not remotely lucid, so at first all I know is that this Man is the most important person around; I don't recognize Him as my Lord, not yet. But as He watches me walk by with my sister, and seems to recognize me, I am compelled to address him. I don't feel important enough to know him, and sincerely hope I'm not only imagining how He looked at me.

Turning back to face him, I say deferentially, "We met earlier" and explain that my sister and I are looking for my grandmother. I tell Him how Abuela was waiting for us, but then suddenly disappeared. I pour the whole story out to him, describing how we walked back to the car looking for her, then into the restaurant beside it, before trying to reach her by phone, all to no avail.

He asks me, "Are you sure she didn't just go to a nearby theater?"

"No!" I reply fervently. "She would never do that!" meaning she would never just abandon us like that.

Leaving my sister behind, we begin walking together, and I can scarcely believe He's actually going to help us. My distress remains intense, but now I feel there is actually hope of finding my lost grandmother. We walk for a time, side by side, very close to each other. Then we seem to pass through a glass partition, something like a door, but I don't remember it opening; we are simply now on the other side.

As we continue walking, drawing ever closer to each other, I become semi-lucid. "My Lord," I ask him, "how can you love everyone the same?"

He replies, "I *don't* love everyone the same."

Clutching tightly to the exposed part of His right arm with both hands, skin to skin, I look away from Him, thinking about His response. I feel His love for me, and how the love that exists between us is unique, because I am unique. With no one else does He feel how He feels with me. I know this is so, and I think —*Just a closer walk with Thee...* He is here with me, as close as we can be, and yet we are are also drawing ever closer...

Abruptly, I arrive home, still not having found Abuela! A woman in a hooded cloak is sitting in my office chair, but she rises as I hurry toward my bedroom. I don't have time to wonder about her because she is not Abuela, who is still missing! The dark-haired stranger gazes at me with gentle concern, a deep compassion in her eyes, but I don't understand who she is, or why she's here, except that her vigil in my study also seems related to Abuela.

I am weeping as I enter the bedroom, where I find my brother.

My emotions are a veritable tempest of despair. Where is Abuela?! I've lost Abuela! We've all lost her! I feel I could deal with life's other problems, if I could only know where my grandmother went, and that she's all right...

I wake up slowly, and the first thing I remember is being with my Lord. At once, the dream's burning despair begins extinguishing itself beneath the balm of His Love. He came to me in a dream again! He appeared to me in the midst of last night's challenging drama, and His Presence, His love, resolved it. Because we *are* loved, we *are* cared for, and no one can ever be lost who does not choose to be. Then I get the distinct impression that Abuela willingly played a part in the night's melodrama, which would make the local theater my Lord suggested she might have gone to my own dream! Despite our differences, Abuela loved me deeply, and I loved her, and our relationship continues in dreams. And I dreamed this on her birthday! Certainly she knows now how much I truly love her!

I drift off again, and dream I'm sleeping with Stinger on a blanket spread across the grass close to our statue of Saint Francis. I feel it is near sunrise, and wonder that we've been sleeping out here without any fear. I see our dog walking around with his quick, intent energy, and feel he has been watching over us. Although I glimpse a small group of people quietly walking through the garden up toward the house, I know we have nothing to fear from them, or from sleeping out beneath the sky...

Inside, sitting alone in semi-darkness, I inhabit my emotions while also hovering just outside my own face. I know it's me even though this woman doesn't look much like me; her flesh is older, and her mouth is slightly ajar, as though beginning to open in a cry of despair welling up from within her/me. She is thinking about people in her life who supposedly loved her. Did they really? She is feeling so alone, so sorry for herself as she cries out in her mind—No one can love you like your father!

Remembering Papi, and all his human weaknesses, I question how much even he truly loved me. Then this woman who is also me crosses the border of despair as we wonder—Is there really nothing but this doomed flesh, this isolated physical existence that one day simply ceases to be forever? At this point, I shift from looking directly at our face to seeing it from an angle, which is less than a profile, but I clearly perceive the curve of a cheekbone and jaw outlined in a bright white light as I/we resist this bottomless feeling of hopelessness, with the thought—GOD is my loving Father. I wake.

When I shared my first dream with Mami that morning, she wrote:

> "Abuela played hide and seek with you to urgently remind you it was her birthday!"

Indeed, that is something I can well believe she would do, test me in the dream space to see how much I really love her. Very much like my old Abuelita!

The lovely, compassionate woman who was sitting in my study, as though waiting for me, I feel is the Virgin Mary, who

Abuela prayed to every night. Whenever I watched the TV in my grandparents' room, I sometimes looked back at her as she prayed, wondering about her devotion to the small black-and-white image of Mary she kept on her bedside table along with a cross, perhaps on a rosary. She kissed both of them every night before she went to sleep. It seemed strange to me, like a childish superstition, yet I also found it a comforting mystery.

The last time I saw my grandmother's physical form was after she had died, and her corpse was lying in a dark hospital bedroom with its mouth hanging open. In my final dream, I feel I became one with her as, in her last moments alone, she wondered if anyone had ever truly loved her. I can hope now that at the end, she felt as I did in my dream—GOD is my loving Father.

Four nights later, on October 7, I dreamed that Abuelo, her husband, called me on the phone. He sounded very far away, but I could clearly feel his presence, and the happiness in his voice, as he talked to me about my dream with Abuela on her birthday. I laughed and said, "Yes, it was just like Abuela to test my love for her!" He was so very glad about this dream I had with his wife.

I love you, Abuelita!

Get Thee Behind Me Satan

Dream of October 7, 2014

I'm the only pedestrian walking down a city sidewalk during some indeterminate time of day. I can scarcely believe it when I see my Lord, looking strangely thin and not so tall, walking a small dog in my direction. He's wearing a gray jacket with the hood up, as if that might help conceal his identity. He doesn't seem to notice me, even though his shoulder brushes mine as he passes between me and the building on my right.

I murmur awkwardly, "Excuse me, sir," but he doesn't acknowledge me, so I keep walking. What else can I do? I'm no one important, so why should he pay attention to me? Nevertheless, I decide to stop, and lean against the building, facing the sidewalk and the street as if waiting for someone else. Following his dog, he retraces his steps, and I watch him, increasingly dismayed by his unappealing aura, as he walks past me with an agitated stride, muttering too himself.

Abruptly, he does an about face, and as he walks past me yet again, he gestures to his dog and says, "If only they knew how much better off they would be without us."

I think—What?! The exact opposite is true: dogs live to please us, to love us, and to be loved and cared for by us in return.

A small crowd of women gathers on the sidewalk around him, and I watch as he interacts with them. I only remember one thing he says to them, "I can feel my needs."

I can't take it anymore. I walk away, glad to be putting him, and his inexplicably nauseating behavior, behind me. But he follows me, and taking firm hold of my left arm, apparently drops his act as he grins at me, and pulls me toward a short flight of steps leading down into a basement apartment.

His face very close to mine, he says, "Don't you see what I did?

I combined all the parts of your earlier dreams into a story. I even said, *Myneeds.*"

I understand he is telling me that he deliberately merged the two words so they sounded like a name, because he was secretly referring to his need, his desire, for me.

As we walk down the steps, I look directly at his face. I am now fully lucid. Incredible! I am completely here with him, and he is talking to me as casually as if we are actually awake and together in reality. He keeps talking and talking, and I think I will have a hard time remembering everything he says.

Abruptly, just before we enter the underground space, I glimpse my husband over my left shoulder. He is walking down another set of steps into our house, and I suffer a pang of guilty regret that I'm cheating on him with this other man. But I scarcely have time to think as I'm whisked to the back of the room, which is narrow and cramped feeling. He lies down on his back across the low bed, and I kneel on the carpeted floor beside him, resting intimately over his chest, conscious of the slightly rough texture of the dark-brown sweater he's wearing.

He continues talking to me as though I am his special companion, the one person he can confide in. His attitude of exclusive confidentiality confuses me, because I know he is equally intimate with countless other souls. So why does he want me to feel as though I am more special to him than anyone else? It's very strange how he's behaving, like a man with the woman he's secretly in love with, and having an affair with.

He tells me, "There can't appear to be anything between us in public. Anything sexual freaks people out." Then, tossing his head emotionally from side to side, he begins confessing his deepest, most secret feelings to me. "I admit, I wondered if my apostles would miss me after I died." He sighs, then seems to wonder out loud, not giving me time to think, "Why didn't I ask them to work for me, the King of the Jews?" He seems to want me to understand that he was much too kind, and that I too am guilty of the same foolish timidity.

This whole scene doesn't feel right, and I stop listening to him, distracted by a tiny but, from my perspective, disturbingly big particle of half-cooked meat resting on his chest that must have fallen out from between his teeth as he talked. I stare at it a few moments before flicking it away with my fingernail in disgust, and slowly wake.

Immediately, I know I have *not* just been with my Lord. The devil, or one of his clever minions, wanted me to believe I was having an amazingly vivid lucid dream with my personal manifestation of the Holy Spirit, to who I am more special than anyone else. But not for an instant did I feel the all abiding love and joy, indistinguishable from an overwhelming humility, that I always experience in the presence of my Lord. Thrilled by the thought that I was completely lucid with Him, I was easily caught in a web of deceitful flattery.

My soul knew from the start he was not my Lord, but curiosity and vanity kept me in his orbit, wanting to be noticed, even though I didn't feel he was even worth being noticed by. In truth, I was only superficially lucid, but lucid enough to sense something was wrong, to doubt that I was truly with my Lord, and the moment I woke up, I knew I had been deceived. My own vanity and pride led me astray, making it distressingly easy for the devil to toy with me.

Chapter Thirteen – Love in Action

I cannot truly love
and trust myself
unless above all else
I love and trust God
Creator of my life
the apple of His I

The Forces of Light

Dream of October 13, 2014

I'm standing in a large building, once the home of a famous individual from another century, but now a museum exhibit. The study, and perhaps one or more other rooms, have been left intact as a permanent exhibit. However, a remodeling project is underway, various pieces of furniture being taken away, and others brought in. Standing in the center of the activity, I spend a long, drawn-out moment staring over at the painting hanging above the celebrated person's desk, studying it in breathtaking detail.

The man in charge of the renovations stops to talk to me, drawing my attention to elegant chairs, set around a circular wooden table antique in appearance, very fine. The slender high-backed chairs are covered in a loose-fitting, off-white fabric. They are very distinctive, and look comfortable.

I leave the room, and find myself in a foyer of sorts, a space both inside and outside this cathedral-like structure. I've come out here to practice my ability to take flight, and someone, perhaps a woman, reminds me to perform my quick walk first, which will help launch me. When I fail my first few attempts, I look around me and think—Of course I can fly, because this is a dream.

Levitating just above the floor, I glide through an elegantly cluttered room before traversing a spacious hallway that leads me through a door into another room. I think—No more doors! as I open a final blue door, and escape.

All around me the sky is a soft white, as though I'm flying through a cloud. Far, far below me to my right, I see a strip of white beach adjoining an endless expanse of ocean. The light shining on the scene is such a pure bright white, the water glimmers like living liquid silver. I am flying so high, the waves below are only subtle, rippling black shadows. I can just barely distinguish the silhouettes of people, isolated handfuls of them playing in the water.

I think—All I want is to be with my Lord.

I begin loosening the white skirt and wrap-around top I'm wearing, exposing myself to the sensual embrace of the dream. The arousal I experience is not sexual; it is all of me, and smolders steadily, like a banked fire. The sublime ocean view to my right appears to have no beginning or end. To my left, and partially before me, there is only an absolute darkness through which I begin soaring at great speed. It's like flying through a vast, pitch-black cavern. I find it thrilling not to be able to see anything as I imagine my dream body colliding with obstacles, which of course won't hurt or stop me; the thought of them only excites me.

Gradually, the black space begins granulating into an immense black cloud expanding to my right, obscuring some of the luminous ocean view below. I can almost distinguish the soot-like particles in this massive cloud, which begins feeling like a corruption of the darkness, like a manifestation of negative thought-energy, as though each human consciousness is akin to a drop of water in this cloud, to a quantum particle, and the probabilities beginning to collapse around me are not good.

I pray quietly, "Help me, my Lord" and I am gently pulled away from this cloud toward the ocean of light. I can see a clear blue sky now, and sections of the water are are also now a bright blue. I am still moving forward at a great speed, faster and faster, as far below me, where the shore meets the ocean, indescribably magnificent visions begin flowing in my direction. I see the visions clearly, and am filled with such awe, I don't regret realizing I won't be able to remember most of them when I wake up. Even in the dream, these visions fill the "cup" of my brain to overflowing, yet I know it doesn't matter whether or not I will be able to describe them. What matters is that I am seeing these visions, and experiencing their reality.

I remember one of the visions. Never will I forget it. Not far below me are ranks of men driving what look to me like chariots forged of the sun's fiery, orange-gold light. The drivers are ideal figures wearing the same intent, determined expressions on their faces. It's like looking directly at the rising or setting sun as its life-giving power flows into several rows of luminous soldiers who hold no weapons, but who are unmistakably on a mission. They can literally be described as the Forces of Light, and never in my life, awake or in dreams, have I witnessed anything more awe inspiring, more full of glorious, transcendent splendor. I keep pace with the vision, which eventually fades, becoming two silver tracks cutting through the darkness.

I wrote nothing about this dream the next day. I was too awed by the vision of heavenly forces commanding the space where the beach, the physical world, merges with the endless ocean of God, the Life of all life.

I still feel the Cathedral-like structure in which my dream began contained the study of an important figure in the church. I perceive this study as representing all the rooms, rich and poor, stretching back centuries to Christ's resurrection, in which men and women have been inspired to write and communicate His teachings, penning countless words for the joy of sharing, and in the hope of spreading, the Good News.

> The word "Gospel" is derived from an Anglo-Saxon word, "godspel", or "good story" and was substituted for the original Greek word "euaggelion" which first signified "a present given to one who brought good tidings", or "a sacrifice offered in thanksgiving for such good tidings having come". In later Greek uses, it was

employed for the good tidings themselves. That's exactly what God is offering us with the Gospel; "good news" about what he did for us through Jesus Christ.[82]

The renovation taking place in the study seems to relate to my own mind, which continues expanding as I read the early church Fathers, and better understand how narrow-minded and ignorant I actually was about the Christian faith. Our minds are furnished with concepts and beliefs, and mine is definitely undergoing some serious remodeling.

The painting hanging over the desk, which I saw with breathtaking clarity, I feel represents the luminous landscape of Christianity as handed down to us by the apostolic tradition, for the more I read my leaders, the more beautifully detailed, and uplifting to my soul, it becomes.

> Matthew among the Hebrews issues a Writing of the gospel in their own tongue, while Peter and Paul were preaching the gospel at Rome and founding the Church. After their decease Mark, the disciple and interpreter of Peter, also handed down to us in writing what Peter had preached. Then Luke, the follower of Paul, recorded in a book the gospel as it was preached by him. Finally John, the disciple of the Lord, who had also lain on his breast, himself published the Gospel, while he was residing at Ephesus… If we are to believe anyone when it comes to the truth about Jesus, who more than those who lived with him and later died for him? And if anyone should be trusted to know these

shepherds' true teaching, who more than those to whom they entrusted their sheep, many of whom also died for Christ? All Christians, whether they are aware of it or not, depend on apostolic tradition, preserved by the early Church Fathers, every time they pick up their Bibles. It is time that they learn to appreciate and articulate the sound reasons for the confidence they place in the book they hold in their hands.[83]

The four white chairs arranged around the circular table as if for a meeting, strike me as four of the world's major religions. Whatever we believe, it does not change the truth that if humanity and the planet are to survive and thrive, we must all learn to live in the Spirit of Love.

The Embracing Tree

Dream of October 15, 2014—*Saint Theresa of Avila Day*

For a long time, my awareness has been in front of a virtual screen, which takes up most of my field of vision and feels like looking into the depths of the universe. I am interacting with a female voice, listening to her instructions, filling out a questionnaire, and otherwise responding to everything she tells me. The activity is intensely engrossing, so I'm shocked when I press a button and the site abruptly crashes, the screen going black.

The woman says calmly, "Oh-oh, be prepared... wait..." The darkness seems to be rebooting, and something forming in the black depths is gradually moving closer...

Like solidifying smoke, an entirely different site materializes, becoming three-dimensional around me. Suddenly, I'm aware of standing at the junction of two corridors. The one behind me is white and evenly lit, as is the one extending to my left. A few feet away on my right, there is the entrance to a dark space, with two low stone pedestals visible near the entrance. A man as white as marble is standing behind one of the pedestals. The instant he materializes, I think—This is *not* the site I was on. My original site appears to have been hacked, and replaced with this one.

The figure walks around the broken column and "speaks" to me with his animal head, a beast's head with a long snout, and horns curving close to his skull where his ears should be. He telepathically informs me he is a teacher, come to give me further instructions on lucid dreaming. He seems to imply, to want me to believe, he is Robert Waggoner deliberately wearing this dream costume.

Part of me listens, wanting to believe him, but my deepest intuition regards him suspiciously. Something doesn't *feel* right. Something is seriously *off* about this scene. He looks like a Greek statue come to life, complete with a small, marble-white penis hanging limply between his legs. I seriously doubt a true teacher of any kind would expose himself to me like this. Then I wonder if I only imagined seeing his penis as darkness wafts around the lower half of his body. No, he is definitely naked, and casually displaying his limp sex to me. Also strangely disturbing is the way he is pacing back and forth, ostensibly like a lecturing professor, but I suddenly sense the truth—he can't cross the threshold between his dark alcove, and the well lit space in which I'm standing. Which means... which means he can't prevent me from walking away from him. This *has* to be a dream, and now that I'm lucid, I know for a fact I don't trust this entity.

I walk quickly away from the beast-man down the hallway to my left. Through small windows in the doors I pass, I see what look like the offices of university professors. I resist the urge to simply fly through the nearest window, confident I can find the exit. I soon come to a door that leads into one of the largest offices, where I find another door that opens onto the outside world.

I emerge onto a sunny open expanse of bright green grass. Drifting over it contentedly, I sense the presence of a great tree attracting me, drawing me toward it. I don't turn to face it, I simply surrender to a mysterious dream gravity pulling me gently back, and then lifting me up between thick brown branches overflowing with luminous green leaves. I know I won't get snagged on anything, that I will simply keep floating through this great tree for which I feel a deepening affection. And it seems to return the sentiment, for as I come to a stop, I feel it supporting and embracing me from behind, like a living chair against which I relax as contentedly as a child in its parent's lap.

I believe I wake up, and just lay there with my eyes closed, remembering my dream. Or perhaps I *do* wake up before slipping seamlessly back into the dream space, where I am also lying on a bed with my eyes closed. Either way, I'm aware of not being in my waking reality house when, along the corridor just outside the room, I hear a gentle commotion of footsteps as people enter, and head quickly to a room near the back.

After an indeterminate amount of time, I hear children singing, and I seem to know they have arrived early to practice for the morning mass. I lay listening to this marvelous childrens' choir, to their crystal clear voices ringing with innocent, earnest joy as they proclaim, "I just want to be with Christ! I just want to be with Christ!" half of them repeating this refrain, while the other half, in perfect harmony, sing words I can't recall exactly, but their meaning is clear to me: Christ's love is always with us, never abandons us, so naturally we want to be with Him!

I open my eyes to a sunlit room. On a white palette, parallel to the foot of mine, I see my sister lying on her back, but with her head raised slightly as she listens to the singing. I smile to myself, thinking—Of course, she's a musician, so she can really appreciate this. Then I glance to my right as my deceased father sits up on his own palette. I smile at him happily, then spring to my feet and run up a flight of wooden steps to find my dream journal. I wake.

That morning I wrote: It can be said that the goat-headed entity from my first dream was shaped by my mind from daily residue, for example, the new tomb discovered in Greece I had seen photos of a few days before, and by my admiration for

Robert Waggoner's work. But a coin has two sides. This entity used pieces of my consciousness to clothe itself in such a way that it would feel familiar, non-threatening. In the dream, I did not think of him as the god Pan or the devil, I simply sensed he was not who he was pretending to be. He had a Greek statue's ideally sculpted body, and the Greeks prided themselves on their reason—he was appealing to my rational faculties, urging me to ignore how I felt about him, but he could not completely mask his bestial nature.

It seems to me that in the dream space, Juliet's question, "What's in a name?" is answered: "Nothing." Something is what it is, no matter what we name it when we wake up. Whether I choose to call it the devil, and others view it as a negative entity, or a psychological projection, etc. does not change the reality of what we encounter and experience.

Without actually thinking about it, I sensed this devil could not come any closer to me, even while it did its best to make me trust it, to make me listen to it. If I had, as the saying goes, fallen under its spell, I might have crossed the invisible threshold separating us. Less than a year ago, I probably would have done so in obedience to lucid logic—This is a dream, nothing can hurt me, so I should face this dream character, and determine what it wants, how it relates to me, and so on. But feeling the wrongness of the situation, and of this entity, I chose not to engage with it. I did not fear it, for it soon became clear it couldn't move any closer to me. I did not run away from a challenge, I removed myself from a possible threat. In the waking world, no one walks in front of a truck to prove their courage, and in lucid dreams, I don't think I should feel obliged to engage with "persons" I feel I don't trust, especially ones who seem to be disguising themselves as someone else, and who apparently "hacked" into my dream space.

I wonder now if the woman who was instructing me at the beginning of the dream could be the same soul who at the moment is educating me in waking life with her books—Saint Theresa of Avila. On the phone a few days ago, Mami told me that someone had just "coincidentally" made her aware that October 15 was Saint Theresa of Avila day.

A psychiatrist might question the existence of intentional forces outside of our own brains, and suggest I am letting my thoughts and dreams be influenced by Christian doctrine, subconsciously manifesting an archetype to frighten myself, in the process both justifying and reinforcing the dogma I'm buying into, because in reality there is no such thing as the devil. This perspective essentially confines reality to our own limited minds.

For several years after I began lucid dreaming, I remained firmly divorced from Christian doctrine. The devil must have been well pleased then to let me go on as I was doing in my dreams, because I was still lost, and he was confident his hounds —earthly temptations and fears—would continue nipping at me, distracting me, and interfering with my soul's desire to find its way home to Christ. The fiend *did* appear to show me some attention on occasion, usually soon after I dreamed with my Guardian Lord, but it wasn't until I recognized in my heart who my Guardian Lord truly was that the devil seems to have put me on his personal to do list.

Christ's Hospital

Dream of November 4, 2014

A young girl who has just begun her menstrual cycle is placed on a cart in great discomfort. I accompany her into a place that feels like a hospital-clinic, but I lose sight of her as I look around curiously.

I'm standing in a corridor, with people in staff uniforms walking purposefully by. However, the atmosphere differs from the cold, edgy sterility of normal hospitals, and I get the feeling all the people who come here for help are more deeply cared for, and cared about. Through an open door, I see a young black woman lying on an examination table, her face a study in acceptance and trusting patience.

Moving on, I suddenly become aware of not wearing anything from the waist down, but I don't feel all that self-conscious as I loosely hold some cloths over my private parts. I will simply be perceived as another patient, even though I'm not; I feel I'm here to help out. And yet I *will* be staying here.

Ostensibly on my way to secure a bed, I stop to kneel before a little boy sitting up as if in a stroller, and give him water to drink. He's thirsty, but can't drink by himself; I have to hold the cup for him. This is what I'm here to do, help in any way I can, contributing my services however I may.

I continue walking, and come upon a large open space filled with narrow white beds. Behind a partition wall with a beveled glass top, I perceive another row of larger, softer-looking beds bathed in sunlight from the windows behind them. That is where I will reside, where I can gaze outside when I'm not working.

A young male attendant in a plain blue uniform seems to know what I want, and grants me the bed I have my eye on. He then instructs another attendant to give me water whenever I need it; he says I can have all the water I desire. Then, as I'm walking away to my assigned place, I hear him tell me, "I love you."

I stop in my tracks, astonished a complete stranger just told me he loved me so unselfconsciously, so naturally. There was nothing perfunctory or rote about how he said, "I love you." It was a quiet statement of fact, and I could feel he sincerely meant it. When I look back at him, he is already bending over another bed, giving his attention to someone else who needs his help, and I realize with a profound thrill that he is a Christian. This hospital is made possible by Christians expressing God's personal love and care for each of us.

Feeling very content, I continue exploring this hospital run by love. Coming upon a little black boy sitting in a wheelchair, I kneel in front of him, and give him water to drink, very carefully, because he is having problems swallowing. Despite whatever ails him, he's a cheerful little soul, and as I'm leaving, he says, "It's going to be dark soon. I like that, because no one can see when I play with myself."

I laugh, delighted by his childish honesty and utter lack of self-conscious shame. I wake.

That morning I wrote: This is only the second time someone has told me in a dream, "I love you." The first time was in the dream I had in April that transformed my life. When I looked back at the attendant who spoke these words to me, even though he had already turned most of his attention to someone else, I saw he was aware of my confused surprise. He was a good distance away from me, and the ward was softly lit, but I recall the gentle smile on his face as he observed my reaction.

I wonder if it was Him... I *feel* in my heart that He was Christ, the Holy Spirit disguised as just another humble care giver, just another dream character. Yet He wasn't disguising Himself, because the truth is that His love lives in, and through, all of us.

Water was the central element of the dream, giving others water to drink, and being offered all the water I myself desired. There is no limit, no end to, no rationing of God's love. Christ said to his disciples after His resurrection, "So now I am giving you a new commandment: Love each other. Just as I have loved you, you should love each other. Your love for one another will prove to the world that you are my disciples." John 13:34-35[84]

I was a nurse *and* a patient, for none of us are without ailments, both physical and spiritual, and we all have the power to help each other live healthier, happier lives. Some people care for other people's bodies, but that is only one expression of how we can help heal each other in the most profound sense as we strive to emulate Christ and His love for us.

Chapter Fourteen – Thresholds

I am a 21st century anchorite
our mountain home my cells
opening onto the Cathedral
shaped from mist by trees
my window on the world
the monitor of my computer
writing and mailing dreams
on the Holy Spirit at work

Miriam

Dream of December 21, 2014

I become lucid at the very end of the night when I see a woman, who I at first believe to be my childhood friend, Miriam. I know she has traveled overseas to work in poor countries, where she teaches and helps children. I enter the dream while staring at her where she stands in the room adjoining mine. She is leaning over a table, patiently instructing a group of young students, her brown hair shining with golden highlights in the gentle sunlight. I admire her patience, her kindness, her unpretentious dedication to doing good, and how totally fulfilled she appears to be. She strikes me as being very much a saint, and as I watch her, I feel I want to be more like her, but I know I have a long way to go. I also know we are being observed from above, as though we are in a film about where we both are now in our lives compared to where we were in our childhoods.

As she leaves the table of children, approaching the threshold joining our respective spaces, I walk eagerly toward her. Then, with a love and longing that surprises me, I quietly say her name, "Miriam..."

The room in which I am standing is dark, so when she pauses on the threshold between us, the light is behind her, and I cannot see her face.

Again, I whisper her name, "Miriam!"

Although I know she sees me, she does not come any closer, and as I continue moving toward her, I begin waking up, thinking—My childhood friend just happened to have the same name as this woman.

When I shared this dream with Mami that morning, she emailed me:

> "The Aramaic name Mariam comes from the Hebrew Miryam, the name of the mother of Jesus, the Queen of Heaven. She is standing at the door in your dream, reminding you she is the one who takes us to her Son. She is the Star of the Sea, the Door of Heaven."

This was something I did not know consciously. There was some kind of barrier separating us, not a block, simply a threshold I could not yet cross. This was a wonderful Winter Solstice and New Moon dream four days before Christmas!

We scarce remember now that once this name was spoken softly in a time before the Aves rang. Perhaps across some threshold it was said, so casually, by one who called to Her, 'Mary.' Then, She might have turned and come, obedient from where the children played together in the dusk; and no one knew that more was said than just a young girl's name.[85]

My inner Mary is still only a silhouette, but I have glimpsed the Grace to which I can aspire.

Recently in Pakistan, over one-hundred children were gunned down in their school. Shortly before that, four Christian children were beheaded for refusing to convert to Islam because they loved Jesus. In my dream, I knew Miriam had been called overseas to help children, and I saw her gently instructing them in a classroom. I feel very peaceful today sensing in my heart that the murdered childrens' souls are being lovingly cared for.

Just as all my life I have talked to my mother about my relationships with men, so too I can talk to Mary about my deepening relationship with her Son.

Love and Courage

Dream of December 30, 2014

I am a young woman, not conscious of being myself. I am sitting in a slightly elevated area behind a lattice screen, through which I can see people walking by just below me, their heads roughly level with my hips. I recognize the figures that appear from the right and, after passing me, walk sharply away to the left.

Suddenly, a young man with dark hair and strong, handsome features, walks past the screen more closely than anyone else. As I catch sight of Him, he looks directly up into my eyes and says, "I love you." Then He is gone, joining the stream of people heading away from my balcony enclosure.

For a moment, I feel shocked by surprise, until I realize my heart recognizes Him. I know Him, and I loved Him once, but something happened... Yet as if no time has passed at all, I know I still love Him, and that I always have! It doesn't matter now why I gave Him up, because we still love each other!

I make my way down, and hurry after Him, but he has already vanished into the crowd of people moving in both directions down this broad white corridor. Then the dream announces it is ending as I almost literally see credits begin scrolling in the distance. Yet I continue searching the crowd for the young man I now want more than anything, although it is clear I will have to wait until He chooses to come to me again...

I continue having a very long, involved night of dreaming, which climaxes on a plane going somewhere. Vaguely, I feel the destination is Rome. There is really no sense of a plane now, but when strong turbulence hits, I comfort the woman beside me, for she is terrified by it. I realize then that I myself am no longer frightened by the jolting and plummeting of the plane soaring through white, gold-tinged clouds, because if I die, I will fly straight to God. Or so I dearly hope! As the flight and the dream continue, I am conscious of thinking more and more about God, writing and reading about God, knowing and feeling things about God.

Midnight Prayer and the Holy Spirit

Experience of January 7, 2015

Lying on my back, I wake up talking to God, praying for people I love, and each time I address Him, I feel the Holy Spirit rush into my body, a pouring in of energy vibrating my cells. The experience is a little frightening, yet it isn't, because I am open to Him. Then I realize I'm still thinking in terms of God and heaven being "up there" when heaven is actually all around me, and I can *absorb* God.

I think—*Oh my Lord!* each time I open myself to the experience. The sensation is similar to the vibrations of falling asleep consciously, but is also different, like being completely filled through my heart. I feel God responding to my being completely open to Him. I seem to feel the Holy Spirit pouring into my heart, and from there through all of me, in response to my speaking directly to Him.

That morning I wrote: I was lying on my back, and I was also not in the process of trying to fall asleep, instead I had just woken up, two significant differences for me when it comes to my usual way of trying to have an OBE or a WILD. And last but not least, I woke up to the experience in the act of praying, something that has certainly never happened before.

This experience can still be explained as the onset of a potential Out of Body Experience, but last night I felt something more, perhaps because I now feel and believe, with every part of me, that the Truth is a Person—Jesus Christ, the Son of God—and that energy is Spirit, a conscious Spirit, God Himself. I felt a Presence last night, *the* Presence, Who seemingly entered me, and then withdrew, waiting each time for me to open myself to Him again as my fear swiftly ebbed in response to my faith, and absolute trust, in God.

I have never had conscious control of the vibrations and sensations that precede an OBE or a WILD, and last night I was still not controlling anything; it was as though my thoughts and feelings were heard, and respected. It seemed then that God was here with me, and that I physically experienced the presence of the Spirit as I opened myself to Him.

Afterword

The Mystery of Norwich Street

I posted this account on my dream sharing Blog[86] shortly after I began writing this book:

The address 12 Norwich Street came to me in a dream on December 6, 2013, the dream in which I feel I first "met" Sean, one of my current dream partners. In this dream, we were quickly surrounded by a small group of people, all of us working toward the same goal:

I'm outside early in the night waiting for someone, a man. We have set up an assignation through a service. I'm standing on a slight rise near the sidewalk, above an empty street to my left. There is a man standing near me who I feel is waiting with me. A car turns left onto the street, heading toward us. I somehow immediately know it's being driven by the man I'm expecting as I move quickly to the sidewalk and hail him, waving my arm as I cry, "12 Norwich Street!" because if he's looking for that address, he'll know he's found it.

At the time, I had no idea why I cried out the address 12 Norwich. I did a web search, and learned about the Norwich 12 historical sites, which include a Cathedral. I did not know what to make of it, and let it go, until several months later, when it occurred to me that perhaps trying to meet at this address in a dream—an address mysteriously known to me in the dream space without my waking conscious knowledge—would help my partners and I in our intent to dream share. I felt this address might help focus and unify our intents, and aid us in obtaining even better results.

Sean, Tilly and I sought, and found, 12 Norwich Street one night, where the address took the form of a house. But on subsequent nights, Sean and I both saw a Cathedral when looking for this same address. Other dreams with religious symbolism led to a group conversation about the spiritual nature of dream sharing. I felt then that this important discussion was the reason my inner self, my soul, had spontaneously cried out the address 12 Norwich Street in a dream months earlier, because it would help bring a group of lucid dreamers together in the proper spirit and aid in our efforts to dream share.

During this conversation, I felt compelled to do a web search for "Norwich Cathedral" and the first sentence on its Wiki page leaped out at me: *"Norwich Cathedral is dedicated to the Holy and Undivided Trinity."*

Since May of 2014, approximately four months after I referred to the address 12 Norwich in a dream, I have been immersed in the mystery of the Holy Trinity, and how the Holy Spirit has been working in my dreams ever since I began lucid dreaming as a spiritual practice. It came to me as a life-changing revelation one morning that a recurring dream character, who I always thought of as my Guardian Lord, was my personal experience of Christ. Synchronicity then led me to a book by A.W. Tozer, *God's Pursuit of Man*, and for the first time in my life, even though I was raised a Catholic, I began to understand the third member of the Holy Trinity—the Holy Spirit. Discovering that Norwich Cathedral is dedicated to the Holy and Undivided Trinity stunned me with joy, for this Mystery is at the heart of the transformation wrought within me the moment I understood the Holy Spirit had been working in my dreams for years.

At this point, I felt the reasons my dream self had cried out "12 Norwich Street!" had been fully revealed. I was wrong. One night lying in bed reading another book by Tozer, I could scarcely believe it when I saw he had written:

> "…Let me introduce a lady who has been dead for about six hundred years. She once lived and loved and prayed and sang in the city of Norwich, England… she walked with God so wonderfully close… England was a better place because this little lady lived. She wrote only one book, a very tiny book that you could slip into your side pocket or your purse, but it's so flavorful, so divine, so heavenly, that it has made a distinct contribution to the great spiritual literature of the world. The lady to whom I refer is the one called the Lady Julian. Before she blossomed out into this radiant, glorious life… she prayed a prayer and God answered… The essence of her prayer was this: 'Oh God, please give me three wounds; the wound of contrition and the wound of compassion and the wound of longing after God… This I ask without condition'."[87]

Nine months earlier, when I dreamed I cried out, "12 Norwich Street!" I would never have imagined, or believed it if I had been told, that I would soon suffer these three wounds myself. I immediately found out more about Julian of Norwich, whose "little" book *Revelations of Divine Love* was the first book published in the English language to be written by a woman. I had never heard of Saint Julian before, and I felt profoundly encouraged to continue writing my own little book, *this* book. Although it can in no way compare to the Saint's masterwork, I hope it will have a positive effect on its readers by serving to illustrate one way in which we can personally experience how much God loves us through the intimate workings of the Holy Spirit.

> "By taking a summary look at the teaching and practice of the Church Fathers up to the beginnings of the fifth century, we can discern a well-inegrated tradition of dreams and dreamwork and recognize its continuity with that of the Old and New Testament...
>
> "Tertullian... spoke of dreams as one of the *charismata* of God, and believed that dreams and visions were promised to people of his own day just as much as they were to the first apostles.
>
> "Origen... saw dreams as part of God's providence 'for the benefit of the one who had the dream and for those who hear the account of it from him'...

"'Dreams, more than any other thing, entice us toward hope,' wrote Synesius of Cyrene, a fifth century bishop of Ptolemais. 'And when our heart spontaneously presents hope to us, as happens in our sleeping state, then we have in the promise of our dreams a pledge from the divinity.'...

"Saint Jerome made little distinction between dreams and visions... For Jerome, God spoke through visions, whether they occurred during sleep or awake... Jerome agrees with Jeremiah that God can use dreaming as well as prophesying as a vehicle of revelation to a person. Such revelation can be a valuable gift from God if the dreamer's life is turned toward God."[88]

The Holy Spirit is everywhere, and can enter a human heart in any way He chooses, when we are awake or when we are asleep and dreaming; no door of our perceptions is ever closed to Him.

Acknowledgments

I wish to thank my mother, Juana Rosa Pita, for being who she is, and for blessing me with her love, support and wisdom when I am both awake and asleep. The fact that you are my mother and my best friend, Mami, is like a beautiful dream God has blessed me with all my life.

I also wish to thank my brother, Mario A. Pita, and Olivia Strand. They are the first persons ever to read one of my books while I was in the process of writing it, and their feedback was invaluable. I am also very grateful for their help in composing a concise description of the book.

About the Author

See also: **luciddreamsandtheholyspirit.com**

Maria Isabel Pita was born in Havana, Cuba. Her family moved to the U.S. when she was eight months old, and she grew up in Fairfax, Virginia. Reading, writing and history have been her abiding passions ever since she can remember. In college, she majored in World History, and minored in English Literature and Cultural Anthropology. She has traveled extensively, and authored a series of critically acclaimed erotic romances. Maria's most recent works are the historical epic *Truth is the Soul of the Sun-A Biographical Novel of Hatshepsut-Maatkare*, and *A Concise Guide to Ancient Egypt's Magic and Religion*. Maria lives on a mountain top with her husband, Stinger, and their beloved dog, Arthur. A regular contributor to the *Lucid Dreaming Experience* Magazine, Maria invites comments and questions on her lucid dreaming Blog: **lucidlivingluciddreaming.org.** She also continues to actively explore the reality of dream sharing with a small group of dream partners. For more information, please visit **lucidfriendfinder.com/dreamshares**.

End Notes

1. James Martin, *Jesus: A Pilgrimage* Audible Audio Book, Chapter 3
2. Albert Haase, *Athanasius: The Life of Antony of Egypt(Classics in Spiritual Formation)* Kindle Edition, Location 299,306
3. The experience of the transitional state from wakefulness to sleep.
4. A lucid experience associated with perceived consciousness apart from the body occurring at the time of actual or threatened imminent death.
5. Donna-Marie O'Boyle, Catholic Saints Prayer Book OSV Publishing, 2008, page 61
6. Prayer to Saint Michael, The Dominican Manual (Browne and Nolan, Dublin, 1913), pp. 78-79
7. N.T. Wright, *Surprised by Hope: Rethinking Heaven, the Resurrection, and the Mission of the Church*
8. E. Allison Peers, Saint Theresa of Avila, *Autobiography of Saint Theresa*, Kindle Edition, Location 2388-2392
9. *Ibid.*, Locations 4703-4707, 4711-4713
10. http://www.christianitytoday.com/ch/asktheexpert/oct26.html
11. http://christianity.about.com/od/glossary/qt/JZ-Book-Of-Life.htm
12. Inflammation of a tendon, most commonly from overuse but also from infection or rheumatic disease.
13. CARM - Christian Apologetics and Research Ministry, https://carm.org
14. Nicholas of Cusa, *The Vision of God* – Kindle Edition
15. Pope John Paul II, *Theology of the Body in Simple Language,* Kindle Edition
16. N. T. Wright, *Simply Jesus: A New Vision of Who He Was, What He Did, and Why He Matters,* Kindle Edition – Location 2489-2494
17. Alternate translation listed in the New Living Translation's version "I AM the Messiah" along with "I am the Lord."
18. Bro Smith SGS, Saint Theresa of Avila, *Interior Castle,* Kindle Edition, Locations 2109-10, 2468-77
19. E. Allison Peers, Saint Theresa of Avila, *Autobiography of Saint Theresa*, Kindle Edition – Locations 4152-4153, 4182-4182
20. Carl Jung, from a 1937 lecture at Yale University
21. http://lucidfriendfinder.com/dreamshares/sample-page/dream-partners/
22. WILD – Wake Induced Lucid Dream
23. DILD – Dream Induced Lucid Dream
24. Luke 1:37 New Living Translation
25. John 1:50 New Living Translation
26. A. W. Tozer, *Experiencing the Presence of God: Teachings From the Book of the Hebrews,* Kindle Edition – Location 376-386
27. Marcellino D'Ambrosio, *When the Church Was Young: Voices of the Early Fathers,* Kindle Edition, Locations 1756-1766
28. David Limbaugh, *Jesus on Trial: A Lawyer Affirms the Truth of the Gospel,* Locations 146-147, 190-191, 350-351
29. J.C. Cooper, *An Illustrated Encyclopedia of Traditional Symbols,* Thames & Hudson, Ltd., London

30	St. Therese of Lisieux, *Story of a Soul*, Third Edition, Translated from the Original Manuscripts by John Clarke, O.C.D. , ICS Publications, page 158
31	http://lucidlivingluciddreaming.org/wp-content/uploads/2013/10/OBEorLucidDream-MariaIsabelPita1.pdf
32	New Living Translation
33	http://lucidfriendfinder.com/dreamshares/
34	Louis M. Savary, Patricia H. Berne, Strephon Kaplan Williams, *Dreams and Spiritual Growth – A Judeo-Christian Way of Dreamwork*, Paulist Press, 1984, pages 28, 35
35	Robert Waggoner, *Lucid Dreaming: Gateway to the Inner Self*
36	David Limbaugh, *Jesus on Trial: A Lawyer Affirms the Truth of the Gospel*, Kindle Edition, Locations 668-671
37	1 Peter 5:6-8 New Living Translation
38	Bro Smith SGS, Saint Theresa of Avila, *Interior Castle,* Kindle Edition, Location 4330-4333
39	*Ibid.,* Locations 214-15, 219-22
40	https://frtim.wordpress.com/2013/05/30/the-often-overlooked-humor-of-jesus/
41	http://www.amazon.com/Truth-Soul-Sun-Biographical-Hatshepsut-Maatkare-ebook/dp/B002HWRUFW/ref=sr_1_15?s=digital-text&ie=UTF8&qid=1417710318&sr=1-15&keywords=maria+isabel+pita
42	Allen, James P (2005) *The Role of Amun* in *Hatshepsut—From Queen to Pharaoh* (Roehrig, et. al) 84
43	Matthew 2:14-15 New Living Translation
44	www.ancientneareast.net/texts/egyptian/speos_artemidos.html
45	Davis, T.M. (2004) The Tomb of Hatshopsitu
46	http://lucidfriendfinder.com/dreamshares/2014/12/26/fieri-curavit/
47	John 6:34-37 New Living Translation
48	John 8:12 New Living Translation
49	Luke 12:35-38 New Living Translation
50	For a few months in 2013, while I was dream sharing with James Kroll, I moved from our bedroom bed to the guest bed in the Den two nights a week, at around 3:00 a.m., in an effort to become lucid on those specific nights.
51	John 3:16 New Living Translation
52	John 3:6-8 New Living Translation
53	http://godzdogz.op.org/2012/01/christ-crucified-our-bridge-spiritual.html
54	Matthew 18:1-3 New living Translation
55	A.W. Tozer, *Man: The Dwelling Place of God,* Kindle Edition, Location 164-170

56	David Bentley Hart, *The Door of the Sea: Where was God in the Tsunami?* Kindle Edition
57	http://www.abarim-publications.com/Meaning/Harim.html#.VInBWzHF98E
58	http://www.gotquestions.org/fruit-of-the-Holy-Spirit.html
59	Robert Waggoner, *Lucid Dreaming – Gateway to the Inner Self*
60	John 20:22 New Living Translation
61	A.W. Tozer, *God's Pursuit of Man*, Kindle Edition
62	Reuben Archer, *The Person and Work of The Holy Spirit*, Kindle Edition
63	http://lucidfriendfinder.com/dreamshares/2014/03/10/into-moonlight/
64	John Allen, *The Global War on Christians*, from the Introduction
65	Wyatt North, *The Life and Prayers of Saint Padre Pio*, Kindle Edition, Location 455
66	2 Thessalonians 3:3 New Living Translation
67	Albert Haase, *Athanasius: The Life of Antony of Egypt(Classics in Spiritual Formation)* Kindle Edition, Location 368-370
68	J.C. Cooper, *An Illustrated Encyclopedia of Traditional Symbols*, Thames and Hudson Ltd. London, pages 58 & 64
69	Isaiah 40:31 New Living Translation
70	http://en.wikipedia.org/wiki/Four_Evangelists
71	E. Allison Peers, Saint Theresa of Avila, *Autobiography of Saint Theresa*, Kindle Edition, Location 2032-2033
72	Bro Smith SGS, Saint Theresa of Avila, *Interior Castle*, Kindle Edition
73	Julian of Norwich (Sanna Ellyn), *All Shall Be Well: A Modern-Language Version of the Revelation of Divine Love*, Kindle Edition, Location 1247-1249
74	Maria Isabel Pita, *Truth is the Soul of the Sun – A Biographical Novel of Hatshepsut-Maatkare*
75	Marcellino D'Ambrosio, *When the Church Was Young: Voices of the Early Fathers*, Kindle Edition, Location 2643-2648
76	A.W. Tozer, *Mornings With Tozer: Daily Devotional Readings*, Wing Spread Publishers
77	*Godspell*, a musical by Stephen Schwartz and a book by John-Michael Tebelak
78	A.W. Tozer
79	Albert Haase, *Athanasius: The Life of Antony of Egypt(Classics in Spiritual Formation)* Kindle Edition, Location 345-346
80	Pope John Paul II, *Theology of the Body in Simple Language*, Kindle Edition, Location 360-361
81	Julian of Norwich (Sanna Ellyn), *All Shall Be Well: A Modern-Language Version of the Revelation of Divine Love*, Kindle Edition, Location 355-357
82	http://coldcasechristianity.com/2014/what-does-gospel-really-mean/
83	Marcellino D'Ambrosio, *When the Church Was Young: Voices of the*

	Early Fathers, Kindle Edition, Locations 1389-1393, 1414-1423
84	New Living Translation
85	Fr. John W. Lynch, *A Woman Wrapped in Silence*
86	http://lucidfriendfinder.com/dreamshares/norwich-cathedral-the-spirit-of-dream-sharing/the-mystery-of-12-norwich/
87	A.W. Tozer, *Man: The Dwelling Place of God*, Kindle Edition, Locations 1074-1088
88	Louis M. Savary, Patricia H. Berne, Strephon Kaplan Williams, *Dreams and Spiritual Growth – A Judeo-Christian Way of Dreamwork*, Paulist Press, 1984, pages 36, 44, 45

Made in the USA
Middletown, DE
07 March 2016